John Alexander Hill

Stories of the Railroad

John Alexander Hill

Stories of the Railroad

ISBN/EAN: 9783744666756

Printed in Europe, USA, Canada, Australia, Japan

Cover: Foto ©ninafisch / pixelio.de

More available books at **www.hansebooks.com**

STORIES *of the* RAILROAD

by
John A. Hill

New York
Doubleday & McClure Co.
1899

COPYRIGHT, 1898, 1899,
BY
S. S. McCLURE CO.

COPYRIGHT, 1899,
BY
DOUBLEDAY & McCLURE CO.

Contents

	PAGE
An Engineer's Christmas Story	7
The Clean Man and the Dirty Angels	27
Jim Wainwright's Kid	45
A Peg-legged Romance	75
My Lady of the Eyes	97
Some Freaks of Fate	151
Mormon Joe, the Robber	191
A Midsummer Night's Trip	227
The Polar Zone	253

List of Illustrations

"Quick as a flash the Kid had my arm." *Frontispiece*

TO FACE

"I noticed his long, slim hand on the top of the reverse-lever" 22

"It was a strange courting . . . there on that engine".... 70

"We carried him into the depot".............. 100

"He was the first man I ever killed"........... 176

"'Mexican,' said I"......................... 236

"What seemed to be a giant iceberg . . ."...... 282

"A white city . . . was visible for an instant".. 292

An Engineer's Christmas Story

Orders 35.   Ds '7/16 18—
    C&E No. 16 Mn.
    C&E No. 17 Wa.
(13) No. 16 & No. 17 will meet at Mercer
Siding, No. 17 to take siding. No. 18 due to leave
El Monte, December 16th is annulled between
El Monte and Morgan.   (13)
35. C&E 16 Mn.   N.G.B.
    Ok Smith 1210 am. MnB   M.N.B.
35 C&E 17 Wa
    Ok 1211 am. MnB.
35. Eames & Smoke No. 16 Mn. Complete — 1214 am MnB
35 Steele & Roberts No. 17 Wa Complete — 1222 Am MnB

FACSIMILE OF A COMPLETED ORDER AS ENTERED IN THE DE-
SPATCHER'S ORDER-BOOK

STORIES OF THE RAILROAD

AN ENGINEER'S CHRISTMAS STORY

IN the summer, fall, and early winter of 1863, I was tossing chips into an old Hinkley insider up in New England, for an engineer by the name of James Dillon. Dillon was considered as good a man as there was on the road: careful, yet fearless, kindhearted, yet impulsive, a man whose friends would fight for him and whose enemies hated him right royally.

Dillon took a great notion to me, and I loved him as a father; the fact of the matter is, he was more of a father to me than I had at home, for my father refused to be comforted when I took to railroading, and I could not see him more than two or three times a year at the most—so when I wanted advice I went to Jim.

I was a young fellow then, and being without a home at either end of the run, was likely to drop into pitfalls. Dillon saw this long before I did. Before I had been with him three months, he told me one day, coming in, that it was against his principles to teach locomotive-running to a young man who was likely to turn out a drunkard or gambler and disgrace the profession, and he added that I had better pack up my duds and come up to his house and let "mother" take care of me—and I went.

I was not a guest there: I paid my room-rent and board just as I should have done anywhere else, but I had all the comforts of a home, and enjoyed a thousand advantages that money could not buy. I told Mrs. Dillon all my troubles, and found kindly sympathy and advice; she encouraged me in all my ambitions, mended my shirts, and went with me when I bought my clothes. Inside of a month, I felt like one of the family, called Mrs. Dillon "mother," and blessed my lucky stars that I had found them.

Dillon had run a good many years, and

was heartily tired of it, and he seldom passed a nice farm that he did not call my attention to it, saying: "Jack, now there's comfort; you just wait a couple of years—I've got my eye on the slickest little place, just on the edge of M——, that I am saving up my pile to buy. I'll give you the 'Roger William' one of these days, Jack, say good evening to grief, and me and mother will take comfort. Think of sleeping till eight o'clock, —and no poor steamers, Jack, no poor steamers!" And he would reach over, and give my head a gentle duck as I tried to pitch a curve to a front corner with a knot: those Hinkleys were powerful on cold water.

In Dillon's household there was a "system" of financial management. He always gave his wife just half of what he earned; kept ten dollars for his own expenses during the month, out of which he clothed himself; and put the remainder in the bank. It was before the days of high wages, however, and even with this frugal management, the bank account did not grow rapidly. They owned the house in which they lived, and out of her half "mother" had to pay all the household expenses and taxes, clothe herself and two children, and send the children to school. The oldest, a girl of some sixteen years, was away at normal school, and the boy, about thirteen or fourteen, was at home, going to the public school and wearing out more clothes than all the rest of the family.

Dillon told me that they had agreed on the financial plan followed in the family before their marriage, and he used to say that for the life of him he did not see how "mother" got along so well on the allowance. When he drew a small month's pay he would say to me, as we walked home: "No cream in the coffee this month, Jack." If it was unusually large, he would say: "Plum duff and fried chicken for a Sunday dinner." He insisted that he could detect the rate of his pay in the food, but this was not true—it was his kind of fun. "Mother" and I were fast friends. She became my banker, and when I wanted an extra dollar, I had to ask her for it and tell what I wanted it for, and all that.

Along late in November, Jim had to make an extra one night on another engine, which left me at home alone with "mother" and the boy—I had never seen the girl—and after swearing me to be both deaf, dumb, and blind, "mother" told me a secret. For ten years she had been saving money out of her allowance, until the amount now reached nearly $2,000. She knew of Jim's life ambition to own a farm, and she had the matter in hand, if I would help her. Of course I was head over heels into the scheme at once. She wanted to buy the farm near M——, and give Jim the deed for a Christmas present; and Jim mustn't even suspect.

Jim never did.

The next trip I had to buy some underclothes: would "mother" tell me how to pick out pure wool? Why, bless your heart, no, she wouldn't, but she'd just put on her things and go down with me. Jim smoked and read at home.

We went straight to the bank where Jim kept his money, asked for the President, and let him into the whole plan. Would he take

$2,100 out of Jim's money, unbeknown to Jim, and pay the balance of the price of the farm over what "mother" had?

No, he would not; but he would advance the money for the purpose—have the deeds sent to him, and he would pay the price—that was fixed.

Then I hatched up an excuse and changed off with the fireman on the M—— branch, and spent the best part of two lay-overs fixing up things with the owner of the farm and arranging to hold back the recording of the deeds until after Christmas. Every evening there was some part of the project to be talked over, and "mother" and I held many whispered conversations. Once Jim, smiling, observed that, if I had any hair on my face, he would be jealous.

I remember that it was on the 14th day of December, 1863, that payday came. I banked my money with "mother," and Jim, as usual, counted out his half to that dear old financier.

"Uncle Sam'd better put that 'un in the hospital," observed Jim, as he came to a ragged ten-dollar bill. "Goddess of Liberty pretty near got her throat cut there; guess some reb has had hold of her," he continued, as he held up the bill. Then laying it down, he took out his pocket-book and cut off a little three-cornered strip of pink court-plaster, and made repairs on the bill.

"Mother" pocketed her money greedily, and before an hour I had that very bill in my pocket to pay the recording fees in the courthouse at M——.

The next day Jim wanted to use more money than he had in his pocket, and asked me to lend him a dollar. As I opened my wallet to oblige him, that patched bill showed up. Jim put his finger on it, and then turning me around towards him, he said: "How came you by that?"

I turned red—I know I did—but I said, cool enough, " 'Mother' gave it to me in change."

"That's a lie," he said, and turned away.

The next day we were more than two-thirds of the way home before he spoke; then, as I straightened up after a fire, he said: "John Alexander, when we get in, you go to Aleck (the foreman) and get changed to some other engine."

There was a queer look on his face; it was not anger, it was not sorrow—it was more like pain. I looked the man straight in the eye, and said: "All right, Jim; it shall be as you say—but, so help me God, I don't know what for. If you will tell me what I have done that is wrong, I will not make the same mistake with the next man I fire for."

He looked away from me, reached over and started the pump, and said: "Don't you know?"

"No, sir, I have not the slightest idea."

"Then you stay, and I'll change," said he, with a determined look, and leaned out of the window, and said no more all the way in.

I did not go home that day. I cleaned the "Roger William" from the top of that mountain of sheet-iron known as a wood-burner stack to the back casting on the tank, and tried to think what I had done wrong, or not done at all, to incur such displeasure from Dillon. He was in bed when I went to the house that evening, and I did not see him until breakfast. He was in his usual spirits there, but on the way to the station, and all day long, he did not speak to me. He noticed the extra cleaning, and carefully avoided tarnishing any of the cabfittings;—but that awful quiet! I could hardly bear it, and was half sick at the trouble, the cause of which I could not understand. I thought that, if the patched bill had anything to do with it, Christmas morning would clear it up.

Our return trip was the night express, leaving the terminus at 9:30. As usual, that night I got the engine out, oiled, switched out the cars, and took the train to the station, trimmed my signals and headlight, and was all ready for Jim to pull out. Nine o'clock came, and no Jim; at 9:10 I sent to his boarding-house. He had not been there. He did not come at leaving time—he did not come at all. At ten o'clock the conductor sent to the engine-house for another engineer, and at 10:45, instead of an engineer, a fireman came, with orders for John Alexander to run the "Roger William" until further orders,—I never fired a locomotive again.

I went over that road the saddest-hearted man that ever made a maiden trip. I hoped there would be some tidings of Jim at home—there were none. I can never forget the blow it was to "mother;" how she braced up on account of her children—but oh, that sad face! Christmas came, and with it the daughter, and then there were two instead of one: the boy was frantic the first day, and playing marbles the next.

Christmas day there came a letter. It was from Jim—brief and cold enough—but it was such a comfort to "mother." It was directed to Mary J. Dillon, and bore the New York post-mark. It read:

"Uncle Sam is in need of men, and those who lose with Venus may win with Mars. Enclosed papers you will know best what to do with. Be a mother to the children—you have *three* of them.

"JAMES DILLON."

He underscored the three—he was a mystery to me. Poor "mother!" She declared that no doubt "poor James's head was affected." The papers with the letter were a will, leaving her all, and a power of attorney, allowing her to dispose of or use the money in the bank. Not a line of endearment or love for that faithful heart that lived on love, asked only for love, and cared for little else.

That Christmas was a day of fasting and prayer for us. Many letters did we send, many advertisements were printed, but we never got a word from James Dillon, and Uncle Sam's army was too big to hunt in. We were a changed family: quieter and more tender of one another's feelings, but changed.

In the fall of '64 they changed the runs around, and I was booked to run in to M——. Ed, the boy, was firing for me. There was no reason why "mother" should stay in Boston, and we moved out to the little farm. That daughter, who was a second "mother" all over, used to come down to meet us at the station with the horse, and I talked "sweet" to her; yet at a certain point in the sweetness I became dumb.

Along in May, '65, "mother" got a package from Washington. It contained a tintype of herself; a card with a hole in it (made evidently by having been forced over a button), on which was her name and the old address in town; then there was a ring and a saber, and on the blade of the saber was etched, "Presented to Lieutenant Jas. Dillon, for bravery on the field of battle." At the bottom of the parcel was a note in a strange hand, saying simply, "Found on the body of Lieutenant Dillon after the battle of Five Forks."

Poor "mother!" Her heart was wrung again, and again the scalding tears fell. She never told her suffering, and no one ever knew what she bore. Her face was a little sadder and sweeter, her hair a little whiter—that was all.

I am not a bit superstitious—don't believe in signs or presentiments or prenothings—but when I went to get my pay on the 14th day of December, 1866, it gave me a little start to find in it the bill bearing the chromo of the Goddess of Liberty with the little three-cornered piece of court-plaster that Dillon had put on her wind-pipe. I got rid of it at once, and said nothing to "mother" about it; but I kept thinking of it and seeing it all the next day and night.

On the night of the 16th, I was oiling around my Black Maria to take out a local leaving our western terminus just after dark, when a tall, slim old gentleman stepped up to me and asked if I was the engineer. I don't suppose I looked like the president: I confessed, and held up my torch, so I could see his face—a pretty tough-looking face. The white mustache was one of that military kind, reinforced with whiskers on the right and left flank of the mustache proper. He wore glasses, and one of the lights was ground glass. The right cheek-bone was crushed in, and a red scar extended across the eye and cheek; the scar looked blue around the red line because of the cold.

"I used to be an engineer before the war," said he. "Do you go to Boston!"

"No, to M——."

"M——! I thought that was on a branch."

"It is, but is now an important manufacturing point, with regular trains from there to each end of the main line."

"When can I get to Boston?"

"Not till Monday now; we run no through Sunday trains. You can go to M—— with me to-night, and catch a local to Boston in the morning."

He thought a minute, and then said, "Well, yes; guess I had better. How is it for a ride?"

"Good; just tell the conductor that I told you to get on."

"Thanks; that's clever. I used to know a soldier who used to run up in this country," said the stranger, musing. "Dillon; that's it, Dillon."

"I knew him well," said I. "I want to hear about him."

"Queer man," said he, and I noticed he was eying me pretty sharp.

"A good engineer."

"Perhaps," said he.

I coaxed the old veteran to ride on the engine—the first coal-burner I had had. He seemed more than glad to comply. Ed was as black as a negro, and swearing about coal-burners in general and this one in particular, and made so much noise with his fire-irons after we started, that the old man came over and sat behind me, so as to be able to talk.

The first time I looked around after getting out of the yard, I noticed his long slim hand on the top of the reverse-lever. Did you ever notice how it seems to make an ex-engineer feel better and more satisfied to get his hand on the reverse-lever and feel the life-throbs of the great giant under him? Why, his hand goes there by instinct—just as an ambulance surgeon will feel for the heart of the boy with a broken leg.

I asked the stranger to "give her a whirl," and noticed with what eager joy he took hold of her. I also observed with surprise that he seemed to know all about "four-mile hill," where most new men got stuck. He caught me looking at his face, and touching the scar, remarked: "A little love pat, with the compliments of Wade Hampton's men." We talked on a good many subjects, and got pretty well acquainted before we were over the division, but at last we seemed talked out.

"Where does Dillon's folks live now?" asked the stranger, slowly, after a time.

"M——," said I.

He nearly jumped off the box. "M——? I thought it was Boston!"

"Moved to M——."

"What for?"

"Own a farm there."

"Oh, I see; married again?"

"No."

"No!"

"Widow thought too much of Jim for that."

"No!"

"Yes."

"Er—what became of the young man that they—er—adopted?"

"Lives with 'em yet."

"So!"

Just then we struck the suburbs of M——, and, as we passed the cemetery, I pointed to

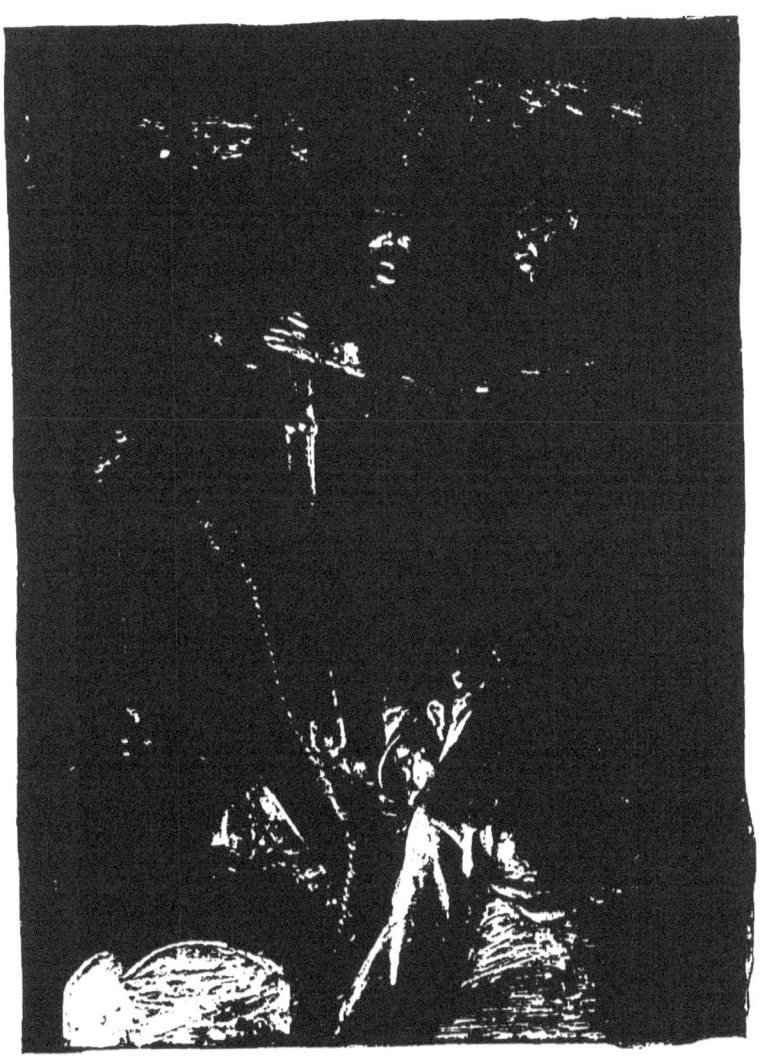

"*I noticed his long, slim hand on the top of the reverse-lever.*"
(*page* 21.)

a high shaft, and said: "Dillon's monument."

"Why, how's that?"

"Killed at Five Forks. Widow put up monument."

He shaded his eyes with his hand, and peered through the moonlight for a minute.

"That's clever," was all he said.

I insisted that he go home with me. Ed took the Black Maria to the house, and we took the street cars for it to the end of the line, and then walked. As we cleaned our feet at the door, I said: "Let me see, I did not hear your name?"

"James," said he, "Mr. James."

I opened the sitting-room door, and ushered the stranger in.

"Well, boys," said "mother," slowly getting up from before the fire and hurriedly taking a few extra stitches in her knitting before laying it down to look up at us, "you're early."

She looked up, not ten feet from the stranger, as he took off his slouched hat and brushed back the white hair. In another minute her arms were around his neck, and she was murmuring "James" in his ear, and I, like a dumb fool, wondered who told her his name.

Well, to make a long story short, it was James Dillon himself, and the daughter came in, and Ed came, and between the three they nearly smothered the old fellow.

You may think it funny he didn't know me, but don't forget that I had been running for three years—that takes the fresh off a fellow; then, when I had the typhoid, my hair laid off, and was never reinstated, and when I got well, the whiskers—that had always refused to grow—came on with a rush, and they were red. And again, I had tried to switch with an old hook-motion in the night and forgot to take out the starting-bar, and she threw it at me, knocking out some teeth; and taking it altogether, I was a changed man.

"Where's John?" he said finally.

"Here," said I.

"No!"

"Yes."

He took my hand, and said, "John, I left all that was dear to me once, because I was jealous of you. I never knew how you came to have that money or why, and don't want to.. Forgive me."

"That is the first time I ever heard of that," said "mother."

"I had it to buy this farm for you—a Christmas present—if you had waited," said I.

"That is the first time I ever heard of that," said he.

"And you might have been shot," said "mother," getting up close.

"I tried my darndest to be. That's why I got promoted so fast."

"Oh, James!" and her arms were around his neck again.

"And I sent that saber home myself, never intending to come back."

"Oh, James, how could you!"

"Mother, how can you forgive me?"

"Mother," was still for a minute, looking at the fire in the grate. "James, it is late in life to apply such tests, but love is like gold;

ours will be better now—the dross has been burned away in the fire. I did what I did for love of you, and you did what you did for love of me; let us all commence to live again in the old way," and those arms of hers could not keep away from his neck.

Ed went out with tears in his eyes, and I beckoned the daughter to follow me. We passed into the parlor, drew the curtain over the doorway—and there was nothing but that rag between us and heaven.

The Clean Man and the Dirty Angels

THE CLEAN MAN AND THE DIRTY ANGELS

WHEN I first went firing, down in my native district, where Bean is King, there was a man on the road pulling a mixed train, by the name of Clark—'Lige Clark.

Being only a fireman, and a new one at that, I did not come very much in contact with Clark, or any of the other engineers, excepting my own—James Dillon.

'Lige Clark was a character on the road; everybody knew "old 'Lige;" he was liked and respected, but not loved; he was thought puritanical, or religious, or cranky, by some, yet no one hated him, or even had a strong dislike for him.

His honesty and straightforwardness were proverbial. He was always in charge of the funds of every order he belonged to, as well as of the Sunday-school and church.

He was truthful to a fault, but above all, just.

" 'Cause 'tain't right, that's why," was his way of refusing to do a thing, and his argument against others doing it.

After I got to running, I saw and knew more of 'Lige, and I think, perhaps, I was as much of a friend as he ever had. We never were chums. I never went to his house, and he never went to mine; we were simply roundhouse acquaintances; used to talk engine a little, but usually talked about children—'Lige had four, and always spoke about "doing the right thing by them."

'Lige had a very heavy full beard, that came clear up to his eyes, and a mass of wavy hair—all iron grey. His eyes were steel grey, and matched his hair, and he had a habit of looking straight at you when he spoke.

On his engine he invariably ran with his head out of the side window, rain or shine, and always bareheaded. When he stepped upon the footboard, he put his hat away with his clothes, and there it stayed. He was never known to wear a cap, excepting in the coldest weather.

Once in a while, when I was firing, I have seen him come in, in winter, with his beard white with frost and ice, and some smoke-shoveling wit dubbed him Santa Claus.

'Lige had a way of looking straight ahead and thinking of his work, and, after he got to running express, would go through a town, where other trains were side-tracked for him, looking at the track ahead, and at the trains, but never seeming to care that they were there, never nodding or waving a hand. Once in a while he would blink his eyes,—that was all. The wind tossed his mane and hair and made him look for all the world like a lion, who looks at, but appears to care nothing for the crowds around his den. Someone noticed the comparison, and dubbed him "The Lion," and the name clung to him. He was spoken of as "Old 'Lige, the Lion." Just why he was called old, I don't know—he was little more than forty then.

When the men on the road had any grievances, they always asked 'Lige to "go and see the old man." 'Lige always went to lodge and to meetings of the men, but was never known to speak. When the demands were drawn up and presented to him, he always got up and said: "Them air declarations ain't right, an' I wouldn't ask any railroad to grant 'em;" or, "The declarations are right. Of course I'll be glad to take 'em."

When old 'Lige declined to bear a grievance it was modified or abandoned; and he never took a request to headquarters that was not granted—until the strike of '77.

When the war broke out, 'Lige was asked to go, and the railroad boys wanted him to be captain of a company of them; but he declined, saying that slavery was wrong and should be crushed, but that he had a sickly wife and four small children depending on his daily toil for bread, and it wouldn't be right to leave 'em unprovided for. They drafted him later, but he still said it "wa'n't right" for him to go, and paid for a substitute. But three months later his father-in-law died, up in the country somewhere, and left his wife some three thousand dollars, and 'Lige enlisted the next day, saying "'Tain't right for any man to stay that can be spared; slavery ain't right; it must be stopped." He served as a private until it was stopped.

Shortly after the war 'Lige was pulling the superintendent over the road, when he struck a wagon, killing the driver, who was a farmer, and hurting his wife. The woman afterward sued the road, and 'Lige was called as a witness for the company. He surprised everybody by stating that the accident was caused by mismanagement of the road, and explained as follows: "I pull the regular Atlantic express, and should have been at the crossing where the accident occurred, an hour later than I was; but Mr. Doe, our superintendent, wanted to come over the road with his special car, and took my engine to pull him, leaving a freight engine to bring in the express. Mr. Doe could have rode on the regular train, or could have had his car put into the train, instead of putting the company to the expense of hauling a special, and kept the patrons of the road from slow and poor service. We ran faster than there was any use of, and Mr. Doe went home when he got in, showing that there was no urgent call for his presence at this end of the line. If there had been no extra train on the road this farmer wouldn't have been killed: 'twa'n't right."

The widow got pretty heavy damages, and the superintendent tried to discharge 'Lige. But 'Lige said "'twa'n't right," and the men on the road, the patrons and even the president agreed with him, so the irate super. gave the job up for the time being.

A couple of weeks after this, I went to that super.'s office on some business, and had to wait in the outer pen until "His Grace" got through with someone else. The transom over the door to the "Holy of Holies" was open, and I heard the well-known voice of 'Lige "the Lion".

"Now, there's another matter, Mr. Doe, that perhaps you'll say is none of my business, but 'tain't right, and I'm going to speak about it. You're hanging around the yards and standing in the shadows of cars and buildings half the night, watching employees. You've discharged several yardmen, and I want to tell you that a lot of the roughest of them are laying for you. My advice to you is to go home from the office. They'll hurt you yet. 'Tain't right for one man to know that another is in danger without warning him, so I've done it; 'twouldn't be right for them to hurt you. You're not particularly hunting them but me, but you won't catch me."

Mr. Doe assured "the Lion" that he could take care of himself, and two nights later got sand-bagged, and had about half his ribs kicked loose, over back of the scale house.

When the trouble commenced in '77, old 'Lige refused to take up a request for increase of pay, to headquarters; said the road could afford to keep us just where we were, which was more than some roads were doing, and "'twa'n't right" to ask for more. Two months later they cut us ten per cent., and offered to pay half script. Old 'Lige

Read — John 3:16

said "'twa'n't right," and he'd strike afore he'd stand it;—and, in the end, we all struck.

The fourth day after the strike commenced I met 'Lige, and he asked me where I was going to hunt work. I told him I was going back when we won. He laughed, and said there wa'n't much danger of any of us going back; we were beat; mail trains all running, etc. "'Tain't right, Brother John, to loaf longer'n you can help. I'm goin' out West to-morrer"—and he went.

Some weeks afterward Joe Johnson and I concluded that, contrary to all precedent, the road was going to run without us, and we also went West; but by that time the country was full of men just like us. When I did get a job, it was drying sand away out at the front on one of the new roads. The first engine that come up to the sand house had a familiar look, even with a boot-leg stack that was fearfully and wonderfully made. There was a shaggy head sticking out of the side window, and two cool grey eyes blinked at me, but didn't seem to see me; yet a cheery voice from under the beard said: "Hello, Brother John, you're late, but guess you'll catch on pretty quick. There's lots of 'em here that don't know nothin' about railroading, as far as I can see, and they're running engines, too. 'Tain't right."

The little town was booming, and 'Lige invested in lots, and became interested in many schemes to benefit the place and make money. He had been a widower for some years, and with one exception his children were doing for themselves, and that one was with his sister, and well cared for. 'Lige had considerable means, and he brought it all West. He personally laid the corner-stone of the courthouse, subscribed more than any other working man to the first church, and was treasurer of half the institutions in the village. He ought to have quit the road, but he wouldn't; but did compromise on taking an easy run on a branch.

'Lige was behind a benevolent scheme to build a hospital, to be under the auspices of the church society, and to it devoted not a little time and energy. When the constitution and by-laws were drawn up, the more liberal of the trustees struck a snag in old 'Lige. He was bound that the hospital should not harbor people under the influence of liquor, or fallen women. 'Lige was very bitter against prostitution. "It is the curse of civilization," he often said. "Prostitutes ruin ten men where whiskey ruins one. They stand in the path of every young man in the country, gilded tempters of virtue, honesty and manhood; 'tain't right that they should be allowed in the country." If you attributed their existence to man's passions, inhumanity or cruelty, or woman's weakness, he checked you at once.

"Every woman that becomes a crooked woman does so from choice; she needn't to if she didn't want to. The way to stop prostitution is for every honest man and woman to refuse to have anything to do with them in any way, or with those who do recognize them. 'Tain't right."

In this matter 'Lige Clark had no sympathy nor charity. "'Twa'n't right"—and that settled it as far as he was concerned.

The ladies of the church sided with old

'Lige in his stand on the hospital board, but the other two men wanted the doors of the institution to be opened to all in need of medical attention or care, regardless of who they were or what caused their ailment. 'Lige gave in on the whiskey, but stood out resolutely against the soiled doves, and so matters stood until midwinter.

Half the women in the town were outcasts from society—two dance-houses were in full blast—and 'Lige soon became known to them and their friends as the "Prophet Elijah, second edition."

The mining town over the hills, at the end of 'Lige's branch, was booming, too, and wanted to be the county seat. It had its church, dance-halls, etc., and the discovery of coal within a few miles bid fair to make it a formidable rival.

The boom called for more power and I went over there to pull freight, and 'Lige pulled passengers only. Then they put more coaches on his train and put my engine on to help him, thus saving a crew's wages. Passenger service increased steadily until a big snow-slide in one of the gulches shut up the road. I'll never forget that slide. It happened on the 26th of January. 'Lige and I were double-heading on nine coaches of passengers and when on a heavy grade in Alder Gulch, a slide of snow started from far up the mountain-side, swept over the track just ahead of us, carrying trees, telegraph poles and the track with it. We tried to stop, but 'Lige's engine got into it, and was carried sideways down some fifty or sixty feet. Mine contented herself with simply turning over, without hurting either myself or fireman—much to my satisfaction.

'Lige fared worse. His reverse lever caught in his clothing and before he could get loose, the engine had stopped on her side, with 'Lige's feet and legs under her. He was not badly hurt except for the scalding water that poured upon him. As soon as we could see him, the fireman and I got hold of him and forcibly pulled him out of the wreck. His limbs were awfully burned— cooked would be nearer the word.

The passengers crowded around, but did

little good. One look was enough for most of them. There were ten or twelve women in the cars. They came out slowly, and stood timidly away from the hissing boilers, with one exception. This one came at once to the injured man, sat down in the snow, took his head in her lap, and taking a flask of liquor from her ulster pocket, gave poor 'Lige some with a little snow.

I got the oil can and poured some oil over the burned parts to keep the air from them; we needed bandages, and I asked the ladies if they had anything we could use for the purpose. One young girl offered a handkerchief and another a shawl, but before they were accepted the cool woman holding 'Lige's head got up quickly, laying his head down tenderly on the snow, and without a word or attempt to get out of sight, pulled up her dress, and in a second kicked out two white skirts, and sat down again to cool 'Lige's brow.

That woman attended 'Lige like a guardian angel until we got back to town late that afternoon. The hospital was not yet in shape, so 'Lige was taken to the rather dreary and homeless quarters of the hotel.

As quick as it was known that Elijah Clark was hurt, he had plenty of friends, male and female, who came to take care of him, but the woman who helped him live at the start came not; yet every day there were dainty viands, wine or books left at the house for him—but pains were taken to let no one know from whom they came.

One day a month after the accident I sat beside 'Lige's bed when he told me that he was anticipating quite a discussion there that evening, as the hospital committee was going to meet to decide on the rules of the institution. "Wilcox and Gorman are set to open the house to those who have no part in our work and no sympathy with Christian institutions, and 'tain't right," said he. "Brother John, you can't do no good by prolonging the life of a brazen woman bent on vice."

"Don't you think, 'Lige," said I, "that you are a little hard on an unfortunate class of humanity, who, in nine cases out of ten, are the victims of others' wrong-doing, and stay in the mire because no hand is extended to help them out? Think of the woman of Samaria. It's sinners, not saints, that need saving."

"They are as a coiled serpent in the pathway of mankind, Brother John, fascinating, but poisonous. There can be no good in one of those creatures."

"Oh yes there is, I'm sure," said I. "Why, 'Lige, don't you know who the woman was that gave you brandy, held your head, and used her skirts for bandages when you were hurt?"

Old 'Lige raised up on his elbow, all eagerness. "No, John, I don't, but she wa'n't one of them. She was too thoughtful, too tender, too womanly. I've blessed her from that day to this, and though I don't know it, I think she has sent me all these wines and fruits. She saved my life. Who is she? Do you know?"

"Yes. She is Molly May, who keeps the largest dance-house in Cascade City. She makes lots of money, but spends it all in charity; there has never been a human being buried by the town since she has been there. Molly May is a ministering angel to the poor and sick, but a bird of prey to those who wish to dissipate."

The hospital was opened on Easter, and the first patient was a poor consumptive girl, but lately an inmate of the Red-Light dance-house. 'Lige Clark did not run again; he became mayor of the little city, had faith in its future, invested his money in land and died rich some years ago.

'Lige must have changed his mind as he grew older, or at least abandoned the idea that to crush out a wrong you should push it from all sides, and thus compress and intensify it at the heart, and come to the conclusion that the right way is to get inside and push out, thus separating and dissolving it. For before me lies the tenth annual prospectus of a now noted institution in one of the great cities of the continent, and on its title page, I read through the dimmed glasses of my spectacles: "Industrial Home and Refuge for Fallen Women. Founded by Elijah Clark. Mary E. May, Matron."

Jim Wainright's Kid

JIM WAINRIGHT'S KID

As I put down my name and the number of the crack engine of America—as well as the imprint of a greasy thumb—on the register of our roundhouse last Saturday night, the foreman borrowed a chew of my fireman's fine-cut, and said to me:

"John, that old feller that's putting on the new injectors wants to see you."

"What does he want, Jack?" said I. "I don't remember to have seen him, and I'll tell you right now that the old squirts on the 411 are good enough for me—I ain't got time to monkey with new-fangled injectors on *that* run."

"Why, he says he knowed you out West fifteen years ago."

"So! What kind o' looking chap is he?"

"Youngish face, John; but hair and whiskers as white as snow. Sorry-looking rooster—seems like he's lost all his friends on earth, and wa'n't jest sure where to find 'em in the next world."

"I can't imagine who it would be. Let's see—'Lige Clark, he's dead; Dick Bellinger, Hank Baldwin, Jim Karr, Dave Keller, Bill Parr—can't be none of them. What's his name?"

"Winthrop—no, Wetherson—no, lemme see—why, no—no, Wainright; that's it, Wainright; J. E. Wainright."

"Jim Wainright!" says I, "Jim Wainright! I haven't heard a word of him for years—thought he was dead; but he's a young fellow compared to me."

"Well, he don't look it," said Jack.

After supper I went up to the hotel and asked for J. E. Wainright.

Maybe you think Jim and I didn't go over the history of the "front." "Out at the front" is the pioneer's ideal of railroad life. To a man who has put in a few years there the memory of it is like the memory of marches, skirmishes, and battles in the mind of the veteran soldier. I guess we started at the lowest numbered engine on the road, and gossiped about each and every crew. We had finished the list of engineers and had fairly started on the firemen when a thought struck me, and I said:

"Oh, I forgot him, Jim—the 'Kid,' your cheery little cricket of a firesy, who thought Jim Wainright the only man on the road that could run an engine right. I remember he wouldn't take a job running switcher—said a man that didn't know that firing for Jim Wainright was a better job than running was crazy. What's become of him? Running, I suppose?"

Jim Wainright put his hand up to his eyes for a minute, and his voice was a little husky as he said:

"No, John, the Kid went away—"

"Went away?"

"Yes, across the Great Divide—dead."

"That's tough," said I, for I saw Jim felt bad. "The Kid and you were like two brothers."

"John, I loved the—"

Then Jim broke down. He got his hat and coat, and said:

"John, let's get out into the air—I feel all choked up here; and I'll tell you a strange, true story—the Kid's story."

As we got out of the crowd and into Boston Common, Jim told his story, and here it is, just as I remember it—and I'm not bad at remembering.

"I'll commence at the beginning, John, so that you will understand. It's a strange story, but when I get through you'll recall enough yourself to prove its truth.

"Before I went beyond the Mississippi and under the shadows of the Rocky Mountains, I fired, and was promoted, on a prairie road in the Great Basin well known in the railway world. I was much like the rest of the boys until I commenced to try to get up a substitute for the link motion. I read an article in a scientific paper from the pen of a jackass who showed a Corliss engine card, and then blackguarded the railroad mechanics of America for being satisfied with the link because it was handy. I started in to design a motion to make a card, but—well, you know how good-for-nothing those things are to pull loads with.

"After my first attempt, I put in many nights making a wooden model for the Patent Office. I was subsequently informed that the child of my brain interfered with about ten other motions. Then I commenced to think—which I ought to have done before. I went to studying *what had been done,* and soon came to the conclusion that I just knew a little—about enough to get along running. I gave up hope of being an inventor and a benefactor of mankind, but study had awakened in me the desire for improvement; and after considerable thought I came to the conclusion that the best thing I could do was to try to be the best runner on the road, just as a starter. In reality, in my inmost soul, my highest ideal was the master mechanic's position.

"I was about twenty-five years old, and had been running between two or three years, with pretty good success, when one day the general master mechanic sent for me.

In the office I was introduced to a gentleman, and the G. M. M. said to him in my presence:

" 'This is the engineer I spoke to you of. We have none better. I think he would suit you exactly, and, when you are through with him, send him back; we are only lending him, mind,' and he went out into the shop.

"The meaning of it all was that the stranger represented a firm that had put up the money to build a locomotive with a patent boiler for burning a patent fuel—she had an improved valve motion, too—and they had asked our G. M. M. for a good engineer, to send East and break in and run the new machine and go with her around the country on ten-day trials on the different roads. He offered good pay, it was work I liked, and I went. I came right here to Boston and reported to the firm. They were a big concern in another line, and the head of the house was a relative of our G. M. M.—that's why he had a chance to send me.

"After the usual introductions, the president said to me:

" 'Now, Mr. Wainright, this new engine

of ours is hardly started yet. The drawings are done, and the builders' contract is ready to sign; but we want you to look over the drawings, to see if there are any practical suggestions you can make. Then stay in the shops, and see that the work is done right. The inventor is not a practical man; help him if you can, for experience tells us that ten things fail because of bad *design* where one does because of bad manipulation. Come up into the drawing-room, and I will introduce you to the inventor.'

"Up under the skylight I met the designer of the new engine, a mild little fellow—but he don't figure in this story. In five minutes I was deep in the study of the drawings. Everything seemed to be worked out all right, except that they had the fire-door opening the wrong way and the brake-valve couldn't be reached—but many a good builder did that twenty years ago. I was impressed with the beauty of the drawings—they were like lithographs, and one, a perspective, was shaded and colored handsomely. I complimented him on them.

"'They are beautiful, sir,' he said; 'they were made by a lady. I'll introduce you to her.'

"A bright, plain-faced little woman with a shingled head looked up from her drawing-board as we approached, shook hands cordially when introduced, and at once entered into an intelligent discussion of the plans of the new record-beater.

"Well, it was some months before the engine was ready for the road, and in that time I got pretty well acquainted with Miss Reynolds. She was mighty plain, but sharp as a buzz-saw. I don't think she was really homely, but she'd never have been arrested for her beauty. There was something 'fetching' about her appearance—you couldn't help liking her. She was intelligent, and it was such a novelty to find a woman who knew the smoke stack from the steam chest. I didn't fall in love with her at all, but I liked to talk to her over the work. She told me her story; not all at once, but here and there a piece, until I knew her history pretty well.

"It seems that her father had been chief

draughtsman of those works for years, but had lately died. She had a strong taste for mechanics, and her father, who believed in women learning trades, had taught her mechanical drawing, first at home and then in the shop. She had helped in busy times as an extra, but never went to work for regular wages until the death of her father made it necessary.

"She seemed to like to hear stories of the road, and often asked me to tell her some thrilling experience the second time. Her eyes sparkled and her face kindled when I touched on a snow-bucking experience. She often said that if she was a man she'd go on the railroad, and after such a remark she would usually sigh and smile at the same time. One day, when the engine was pretty nearly ready, she said to me:

" 'Mr. Wainright, who is going to fire the Experiment?'

" 'I don't know. I had forgot about that; I'll have to see about it.'

" 'It wouldn't be of much use to get an

experienced man, would it—the engine will burn a new fuel in a new way?'

" 'No,' said I, 'not much.'

" 'Now,' said she, coloring a little, 'let me ask a favor of you. I have a brother who is just crazy to go out firing. I don't want him to go unless it's with a man I can trust; he is young and inexperienced, you know. Won't you take him? Please do.'

" 'Why, I'll be glad to,' said I. 'I'll speak to the old man about it.'

" 'Don't tell him it's my brother.'

" 'Well, all right.'

"The old man told me to hire whoever I liked, and I told Miss Reynolds to bring the boy in the morning.

" 'Won't you wait until Monday? It will be an accommodation to me.'

"Of course I waited.

"The next day Miss Reynolds did not come to the office, and I was busy at the shop. Monday came, but no Miss Reynolds. About nine o'clock, however, the foreman came down to the Experiment with a boy, apparently about eighteen years old, and said there was a lad with a note for me.

"Before reading the note I shook hands with the boy, and told him I knew who he was, for he looked like his sister. He was small, but wiry, and had evidently come prepared for business, as he had some overclothes under his arm and a pair of buckskin gloves. He was bashful and quiet, as boys usually are during their first experience away from home. The note read:

"'DEAR MR. WAINRIGHT.—This will be handed you by brother George. I hope you will be satisfied with him. I know he will try to please you and do his duty; don't forget how green he is. I am obliged to go into the country to settle up some of my father's affairs and may not see you again before you go. I sincerely hope the "Experiment," George, and his engineeer will be successful. I shall watch you all.
"'G. E. REYNOLDS.'

"I felt kind of cut up, somehow, about going away without bidding Old Business—as the other draughtsman called Miss Reynolds

—good-by; but I was busy with the engine.

"The foreman came along half an hour after the arrival of young Reynolds, and seeing him at work cleaning the window glass, asked who he was.

" 'The fireman,' said I.

" 'What! that kid?'

"And from that day I don't think I ever called young Reynolds by any other name half a dozen times. That was the 'Kid' you knew. When it came quitting time that night, I asked the Kid where they lived, and he said, Charlestown. I remarked that his voice was like his sister's; but he laughed, and said I'd see difference enough if they were together; and bidding me good-night, caught a passing car.

"We broke the Experiment in for a few days, and then tackled half a train for Providence. She would keep her water just about hot enough to wash in with the pump on. It was a tough day; I was in the front end half the time at every stop. The Kid did exactly what I told him, and was in good spirits all the time. I was cross. Nothing will make a man crosser than a poor steamer.

"We got to Providence in the evening tired; but after supper the Kid said he had an aunt and her family living there, and if I didn't mind, he'd try to find them. I left the door unlocked, and slept on one side of the bed, but the Kid didn't come back; he was at the engine when I got there the next morning.

"The Kid was such a nice little fellow I liked to have him with me, and, somehow or other (I hardly noticed it at the time), he had a good influence on me. In them days I took a drink if I felt like it; but the Kid got me into the habit of taking lemonade, and wouldn't go into drinking places, and I soon quit it. He gave me many examples of controlling my temper, and soon got me into the habit of thinking before I spoke.

"We played horse with that engine for four or five weeks, mostly around town, but I could see it was no go. The patent fuel was no good, and the patent fire-box little better, and I advised the firm to put a standard boiler on her and a pair of links, and sell her while the paint was fresh. They took my advice.

"The Kid and I took the engine to Hinkley's, and left her there; we packed up our overclothes, and as we walked away, the Kid asked: 'What will you do now, Jim?'

"'Oh, I've had a nice play, and I'll go back to the road. I wish you'd go along.'

"'I wouldn't like anything better; will you take me?'

"'Yes, but I ain't sure that I can get you a job right away.'

"'Well, I could fire for you, couldn't I?'

"'I'd like to have you, Kid; but you know I have a regular engine and a regular fireman. I'll ask for you, though.'

"'I won't fire for anybody else!'

"'You won't! What would you do if I should die?'

"'Quit.'

"'Get out!'

"'Honest; if I can't fire for you, I won't fire at all.'

"I put in a few days around the 'Hub,'

and as I had nothing to do, my mind kept turning to Miss Reynolds. I met the Kid daily, and on one of our rambles I asked him where his sister was.

" 'Out in the country.'

" 'Send word to her that I am going away and want to see her, will you, Kid?'

" 'Well, yes; but Sis is funny; she's too odd for any use. I don't think she'll come.'

" 'Well, I'll go and see her.'

" 'No, Sis would think you were crazy.'

" 'Why? Now look here Kid, I like that sister of yours, and I want to see her.'

"But the Kid just stopped, leaned against the nearest building, and laughed—laughed until the tears ran down his cheeks. The next day he brought me word that his sister had gone to Chicago to make some sketches for the firm and hoped to come to see us after she was through. I started for Chicago the day following, the Kid with me.

"I had little trouble in getting the Kid on with me, as my old fireman had been promoted. I had a nice room with another plug-puller, and in a few days I was in the old jog—except for the Kid. He refused to room with my partner's fireman; and when I talked to him about saving money that way, he said he wouldn't room with any one —not even me. Then he laughed, and said he kicked so that no one could room with him. The Kid was the butt of all the firemen on account of his size, but he kept the cleanest engine, and was never left nor late, and seemed more and more attached to me—and I to him.

"Things were going along slick enough when Daddy Daniels had a row with his fireman, and our general master mechanic took the matter up. Daniels' fireman claimed the run with me, as he was the oldest man, and, as they had an 'oldest man' agreement, the master mechanic ordered Smutty Kelly and the Kid changed.

"I was not in the roundhouse when the Kid was ordered to change, but he went direct to the office and kicked, but to no purpose. Then he came to me.

"'Jim,' said he, with tears in his eyes, 'are you satisfied with me on the 12?'

"'Why, yes, Kid. Who says I'm not?'

"'They've ordered me to change to the 17 with that horrible old ruffian Daniels, and Smutty Kelly to go with you.'

"'They have!' says I. 'That slouch can't go out with me the first time; I'll see the old man.'

"But the old man was mad by the time I got to him.

"'That baby-faced boy says he won't fire for anybody but you; what have you been putting into his head?'

"'Nothing; I've treated him kindly, and he likes me and the 12—that's the cleanest engine on the—'

"'Tut, tut, I don't care about that; I've ordered the firemen on the 12 and 17 changed—and they are going to be changed.'

"The Kid had followed me into the office, and at this point said, very respectfully:

"'Excuse me, sir, but Mr. Wainright and I get along so nicely together. Daniels is a bad man; so is Kelly; and neither will get along with decent men. Why can't you—

"'There! stop right there, young man. Now, will you go on the 17 *as ordered?*'

"'Yes, if Jim Wainright runs her.'

"'No *ifs* about it; will you go?'

"'No, sir, I won't!'

"'You are discharged, then.'

"'That fires me, too,' said I.

"'Not at all, not at all; this is a fireman row, Jim.'

"I don't know what struck me then, but I said:

"'No one but this boy shall put a scoop of coal in the 12 or any other engine for me; I'll take the poorest run you have, but the Kid goes with me.'

"Talk was useless, and in the end the Kid and I quit and got our time.

"That evening the Kid came to my room and begged me to take my job back and he would go home; but I wouldn't do it, and asked him if he was sick of me.

"'No, Jim,' said he. 'I live in fear that something will happen to separate us, but I don't want to be a drag on you—I think more of you than anybody.'

"They were buying engines by the hundred on the Rio Grande and Santa Fé and the A. & P. in those days, and the Kid and I struck out for the West, and inside of thirty days we were at work again.

"We had been there three months, I guess, when I got orders to take a new engine out to the front and leave her, bringing back an old one. The last station on the road was in a box-car, thrown out beside the track on a couple of rails. There was one large, rough-board house, where they served rough-and-ready grub and let rooms. The latter were stalls, the partitions being only about seven feet high. It was cold and bleak, but right glad we were to get there and get a warm supper. Everything was rough, but the Kid seemed to enjoy the novelty. After supper I asked the landlord if he could fix us for the night.

" 'I can jest fix ye, and no more,' said he; 'I have just one room left. Ye's'll have to double up; but this is the kind o' weather for that; it'll be warmer.'

"The Kid objected, but the landlord

bluffed him—didn't have any other room—and he added: 'If I was your pardner there, I'd kick ye down to the foot, such a cold strip of bacon as ye must be.'

"About nine o'clock the Kid slipped out, and not coming in for an hour, I went to look for him. As I went toward the engine, I met the watchman:

"'Phy don't that fireman o' yourn sleep in the house or on the caboose floor such a night as this? He'll freeze up there in that cab wid no blankets at all; but when I tould him that, he politely informed meself that he'd knowed men to git rich mindin' their own biz. He's a sassy slip of a Yankee.'

"I climbed up on the big consolidation, and, lighting my torch, looked over the boiler-head at the Kid. He was lying on a board on the seat, with his overcoat for a covering and an arm-rest for a pillow.

"'What's the matter with you, Kid?' I asked. 'What are you doing freezing here when we can both be comfortable and warm in the house? Are you ashamed or afraid to sleep with me? I don't like this for a cent.'

JIM WAINRIGHT'S KID   67

" 'Hope you won't be mad with me, Jim, but I won't sleep with any one; there now!'

" 'You're either a fool or crazy,' said I. 'Why, you will half freeze here. I want some explanation of such a trick as this.'

"The Kid sat up, looked at me soberly for a few seconds, reached up and unhooked his door, and said:

" 'Come over and sit down, Jim, and I'll tell you something.'

"I blew out the torch and went over, half mad. As I hooked the door to keep out the sharp wind I thought I heard a sob, and I took the Kid's head in my hands and turned his face to the moonlight. There were big tears in the corner of each tightly closed eye.

" 'Don't feel bad, Kid,' said I. 'I'm sure there's some reason keeps you at such tricks as this; but tell me all your trouble—it's imaginary, I know.'

"There was a tremor in the Kid's voice as he took my hand and said, 'We are friends, Jim; ain't we?'

" 'Why, of course,' said I.

" 'I have depended on your friendship and

kindness and manhood, Jim. It has never failed me yet, and it won't now, I know. I have a secret, Jim, and it gnaws to be out one day, and hides itself the next. Many and many a time I have been on the point of confessing to you, but something held me back. I was afraid you would not let me stay with you, if you knew—'

" 'Why, you ain't killed any one, Kid?' I asked, for I thought he was exaggerating his trouble.

" 'No—yes, I did, too—I killed my sister.'

"I recoiled, hurt, shocked. 'You——'

" 'Yes, Jim, there is no such person to be found as my sister, Georgiana—*for I am she!*'

" 'You! Why, Kid, you're crazy!'

" 'No, I'm not. Listen, Jim, and I will explain.'

" 'My father was always sorry I was not a boy. Taught me boyish tricks, and made me learn drawing. I longed for the life on a locomotive—I loved it, read about it, thought of it, and prayed to be transformed into *something* that could go out on the road.

My heart went out to you early in our acquaintance, and one day the thought to get started as a fireman with you shot into my brain and was acted upon at once. After the first move there was no going back, and I have acted my part well; I have even been a good fireman. I am strong, healthy, and happy when on the road with you. I love the life, hard as it is, and can't think of giving it up, and—and you, Jim.'

"And then she broke down, and cried as only a woman can.

"I took both her hands in mine and kissed her—think of kissing your fireman on the engine—and told her that we could be happy yet. Then I told her how I had tried to get a letter to the lost sister, and how they never came back, and were never answered—that I loved the sister and loved her. She reminded me that she herself got all the letters I had sent, and was pretty sure of her ground when she threw herself on my protection.

"It was a strange courting, John, there on that engine at the front, the boundless plains on one side, the mountains on the other, the winds of the desert whirling sand and snow against our little house, and the moon looking coldly down at the spectacle of an engineer making love to his fireman.

"That night the Kid slept in the bed in the house, and I stayed on the engine.

"When we got back to headquarters the Kid laid off to go home, and I made a trip or two with another fireman, and then I had to go to Illinois to fix up some family business —Kid and I arranged that.

"We met in St. Louis, the Kid hired a ball dress, and we were married as quiet as possible. I had promised the Kid that, for the present at least, she could stay on the road with me, and you know that the year you were there I done most of the heavy firing while the Kid did the running. We remained in the service for something like two years—a strange couple, but happy in each other's company and our work.

"I often talked to my wife about leaving the road and starting in new, where we were not known, as man and wife, she to remain at home; but she wouldn't hear of it, asking

"It was a strange courting . . . there on that engine." (page 69.)

if I wanted an Irishman for a side-partner. This came to be a joke with us—'When I get my Irishman I will do so-and-so.'

"One day, as our 'hog' was drifting down the long hill, the Kid said to me, 'Jim, you can get your Irishman; I'm going to quit this trip.'

" 'Kind o' sudden, hey, Kid?'

" 'No, been hating to give up, but—' and then the Kid came over and whispered something to me.

"John, we both quit and went South. I got a job in Texas, and the Kid was lost sight of, and Mrs. J. E. Wainright appeared on the scene in tea-gown, train, and flounces. We furnished a neat little den, and I was happy. I missed my kid fireman, and did indeed have an Irishman. Kid had a struggle to wear petticoats again, and did not take kindly to dish-washing, but we were happy just the same.

"Our little fellow arrived one spring day, and then our skies were all sunshiny for three long, happy years, until one day Kid and I followed a little white hearse out beyond the cypress grove and saw the earth covered over our darling, over our hopes, over our sunshine, and over our hearts.

"After that the house was like a tomb, so still, so solemn, and at every turn were reminders of the little one who had faded away like the morning mist, gone from everything but our memories—there his sweet little image was graven by the hand of love and seared by the branding-iron of sorrow.

"Men and women of intelligence do not parade their sorrows in the market-place; they bear them as best they can, and try to appear as others, but once the specter of the grim destroyer has crossed the threshold, his shadow forever remains, a dark reminder, like a prison-bar across the daylight of a cell. This shadow is seen and recognized in the heart of a father, but it is larger and darker and more dreadful in the mother heart.

"At every turn poor Kid was mutely reminded of her loss, and her heart was at the breaking point day by day, and she begged for her old life, to seek forgetfulness in toil and get away from herself. So we went back to the old road, as we went away—Jim Wainright and Kid Reynolds—and glad enough they were to get us again for the winter work.

"Three years of indoor life had softened the wiry muscles of the Kid, and our engine was a hard steamer, so I did most of the work on the road. But the work, excitement, and outdoor life brought back the color to pale cheeks, and now and then a smile to sad lips—and I was glad.

"One day the Kid was running while I broke up some big lumps of coal, and while busy in the tank I felt the air go on full and the reverse lever come back, while the wheels ground sand. I stepped quickly toward the cab to see what was the matter, when the Kid sprang into the gangway and cried 'Jump!'

"I was in the left gangway in a second, but quick as a flash the Kid had my arm.

" 'The other side! Quick! The river!'

"We were almost side by side as she swung me toward the other side of the engine, and jumped as we crashed into a landslide. I felt Kid's hand on my shoulder as I left the deck—just in time to save my life, but not the Kid's.

"She was crushed between the tank and boiler in the very act of keeping me from jumping to certain death on the rocks in the river below.

"When the crew came over they found me with the crushed clay of my poor, loved Kid in my arms, kissing her. They never knew who she was. I took her back to our Texas home and laid her beside the little one that had gone before. The Firemen's Brotherhood paid Kid's insurance to me and passed resolutions saying: 'It has pleased Almighty God to remove from our midst our beloved brother, George Reynolds,' etc., etc.

"George Reynolds's grave cannot be found; but over a mound of forget-me-nots away in a Southern land, there stands a stone on which is cut: 'Georgiana, wife of J. E. Wainright, aged thirty-two years.'

"But in my heart there is a golden pyramid of love to the memory of a fireman and a sweetheart known to you and all the world but me, as 'Jim Wainright's Kid.'"

A Peg-Legged Romance

A PEG-LEGGED ROMANCE

Some men are born heroes, some become heroic, and some have heroism thrust upon them; but nothing of the kind ever happened to me.

I don't know how it is; but, some way or other, I remember all the railroad incidents I see or hear, and get to the bottom of most of the stories of the road. I must study them over more than most men do, or else the other fellows enjoy the comedies and deplore the tragedies, and say nothing. Sometimes I am mean enough to think that the romance, the dramas, and the tragedies of the road don't impress them as being as interesting as those of the plains, the Indians, or the seas—people are so apt to see only the everyday side of life anyway, and to draw all their romance and heroics from books.

I helped make a hero once—no, I didn't

either; I helped make the golden setting after the rough diamond had shown its value.

Miles Diston pulled freight on our road a few years ago. He was of medium stature, dark complexion, but no beauty. He was a manly-looking fellow, well-educated enough, sober, and a steady-going, reliable engineer; you would never pick him out for a hero. Miles was young yet—not thirty—but, somehow or other, he had escaped matrimony: I guess he had never had time. He stayed on the farm at home until he was of age, and then went firing, so that when I first knew him he had barely got to his goal—the throttle.

A good many men, when they first get there, take great interest in their work for a few months—until experience gives them confidence; then they take it easier, look around, and take some interest in other things. Most of them never hope to get above running, and so sit down more or less contented, get married, buy real estate, gamble, or grow fat, each according to the dictates of his own conscience or the inclinations of his make-up. Miles figured a little on matrimony.

I can't explain it; but when a railroad man is in trouble, he comes to me for advice, just as he would go to the company doctor for kidney complaint. I am a specialist in heart troubles. Miles came to me.

Miles was like the rest of them. They don't come right down and say, "Something's the matter with me; what would you do for it?" No, sir! They hem and haw, and laugh off the symptoms, until you come right out and tell them just how they feel and explain the cause; then they will do anything you say. Miles hemmed and hawed a little, but soon came out and showed his symptoms—he asked me if I had ever noticed the "Frenchman's" girl.

"The Frenchman," be it known, was our boss bridge carpenter. He lived at a small place half-way over my division—I was pulling express—and the freights stopped there, changing engines. I knew Venot, the bridge carpenter, very well; met him in lodge occasionally, and once in a while he rode on the engine with me to inspect bridges. His wife was a Canadian woman, and good-looking for her forty years and ten children. The daughter that was killing Miles Diston, Marie Venot, was the eldest, and had just graduated from some sisters' school. She was a very handsome girl, and you could read the romantic nature of her being through her big, round, gray eyes. She was vivacious, and loved to go; but she was a dutiful daughter, and at once took hold to help her mother in a way that made her all the more adorable in the eyes of practical men like Miles.

Miles made the most of his opportunities.

But, bless you, there were other eyes for good-looking girls besides those in poor Miles Diston's head, and he was far from having the field to himself; this he wanted badly, and came to get advice from me.

I advised strongly against wasting energy to clear the field, and in favor of putting it all into making the best show and in getting ahead of all competitors. Under my advice,

Miles disposed of some vacant lots, and bought a neat little house, put it in thorough order, and made the best of his opportunities with Marie.

Marie came to our house regularly, and I had good opportunity to study her. She was a sensible little creature, and, to my mind, just the girl for Miles, as Miles was just the man for her. But she had confided to my wife the fact that she never, never could consent to marry and settle down in the regulation, humdrum way; she wanted to marry a hero, some one she could look up to—a king among men.

My wife told her that kings and heroes were scarce just then, and that a lot of pretty good women managed to be comparatively happy with common railroad men. But Marie wanted a hero, and would hear of nothing less.

It was during one of her visits to my house that Miles took Marie out for a ride and (accidentally, of course) dropped around by his new house, induced her to look at it, and told his story, asking her to make the home complete. It would have caught almost any girl; but when Miles delivered her at our door and drove off, I knew that there would be a "For Rent" card on that house in a few days and that Marie Venot was bound to have a hero or nothing.

Miles took his repulse calmly, but it hurt. He told me that Marie was hunting for a different kind of man from him; said that he thought perhaps if he would enlist, and go out to fight Sitting Bull, and come home in a new, brass-bound uniform, with a poisoned arrow sticking out of his breast, she would fall at his feet and worship him. She told him she liked him better than any of the town boys; his calling was noble enough and hard enough; but she failed to see her ideal hero in a man with blue overclothes on and cinders in his ears. If any of Miles's competitors had rescued a drowning child, or killed a bear with a penknife, at this juncture, I'm afraid Marie would have taken him. But, as I have indicated, it was a dull season for heroes.

About this time our road invested in some

mogul passenger engines, and I drew one. I didn't like the boiler sticking back between me and Dennis Rafferty. I didn't like six wheels connected. I didn't like a knuckle-joint in the side rod. I didn't like eighteen-inch cylinders. I was opposed to solid-end rods. And I am afraid I belonged to a class of ignorant, short-sighted, bull-headed engineers who didn't believe that a railroad had any right to buy anything but fifteen by twenty-two eight-wheelers — the smaller they were the more men they would want. I got over that a long time ago; but, at the time I write of, I was cranky about it. The moguls were high and short and jerky, and they tossed a man around like a rat in a corn-popper. One day, as I was chasing time over our worst division, holding on to the arm-rest and watching to see if the main frame touched the driving-boxes as she rolled, Dennis Rafferty punched me in the small of the back, and said: "Jahn, for the love ave the Vargin, lave up on her a minit. Oi does be chasing that dure for the lasth twinty minits, and dang the wan'st has I hit it fair. She's the divil on th' dodge."

Dennis had a pile of coal just inside and just outside of the door, the forward grates were bare, the steam was down, and I went in seven minutes late, too mad to eat—and that's pretty mad for me. I laid off, and Miles Diston took the high-roller out next trip.

Miles didn't rant and write letters or poetry, or marry some one else to spite himself, or take the first steamer for Burraga, or Equatorial Africa, as rejected lovers in stories do. It hurt, and he didn't enjoy it, but he bore up all right, and went about his business, just as hundreds of other sensible men do every day. He gave up entirely, however, rented his house, and said he couldn't fill the bill—there wasn't a hero in his family as far back as he could remember.

Miles had been making time with the Black Maria for about a week, when the big accident happened in our town. The boilers in a cotton mill blew up, and killed a score of girls and injured hundreds more. Miles was at the other end of the division, and they hurried him out to take a car-load of doctors down. They were given the right of the road, and Miles tested the speed of that mogul—proving that a pony truck would stay on the track at fifty miles an hour, which a lot of us "cranks" had disputed.

A few miles out there is a coaling-station, and at that time they were building the chutes. One of the iron drop-aprons fell just before Miles with the mogul got to it; it smashed the headlight, dented the stack, ripped up the casing of the sand-box and dome, cut a slit in the jacket the length of the boiler, tore off the cab, struck the end of the first car, and then tore itself loose, and fell to the ground.

The throttle was knocked wide open, and the mogul was flying. Miles was thrown down, his head cut open by a splinter, and his foot pretty badly hurt. He picked himself up instantly, and took a look back as he closed the throttle. Everything was "coming" all right, he remembered the emergency of the case, and opened the throttle again. A hasty inspection showed the engine in condition to run—she only looked crippled. Miles had to stand up. His foot felt numb and weak, so he rested his weight on the other foot. He was afraid he would fall off if he became faint, and he had Dennis take off the bell-cord and tie it around his waist, throwing a loop over the reverse lever, as a measure of safety. The right side of the cab and all the roof were gone, so that Miles was in plain sight. The cut in his scalp bled profusely, and in trying to wipe the blood from his eyes, he merely spread it all over himself, so that he looked as if he had been half murdered.

It was this apparition of wreck, ruin, and concentrated energy that Marie Venot saw flash past her father's door, hastening to the relief of the victims of a worse disaster, forty miles away.

Her father came home for his dinner in a few minutes from his little office in the depot. To his daughter's eager inquiry he said there had been some big accident in town and the "extra" was carrying doctors from up the road. But what was the matter with the engine, he didn't know; it was the 170; so it was old man Alexander, he said—and that's the nearest I ever came to being a hero.

Marie knew who was running the 170 pretty well; so after dinner she went to the telegraph office for information, and there she learned that the special had struck the new coal chute at Coalton and that the engineer was hurt. It was time she ran down to see Mrs. Alexander, she said, and that afternoon's regular delivered her in town.

Like all other railroaders not better employed, I dropped round to the depot at train time to talk with the boys and keep track of things in general. The regular was late, but Miles Diston was coming with a special, and came while we were talking about it. Miles didn't realize how badly he was hurt until he stopped the mogul in front of the general office. So long as the excitement of the run was on, so long as he saw the absolute necessity of doing his whole duty until the desired end was accomplished, so long as he had a reputation to protect, his will power subordinated all else. But when several of us engineers ran up to the engine, we found Miles hanging to the reverse lever by his safety cord, in a dead faint. We carried him into the depot, and one of the doctors administered some restorative. Then we got a hack and started him and the doctor for my house; but Miles came to himself, and insisted on going to his boarding-house and nowhere else.

Mrs. Bailey, Miles's boarding-house keeper, had been a trained nurse, but had a few years before invested in a rather disappointing matrimonial venture. She was one of the best nurses and one of the "crankiest" women I ever knew. I believe she was actually glad to see Miles come home hurt, just to show how she could pull him through.

The doctor found that Miles had an ankle out of joint; the little toe was badly crushed; there was a bad cut in the leg, that had bled profusely; there was a black bruise over the short ribs on the right side, and there was a button-hole in the scalp that needed about four stitches. The little toe was cut off without ceremony, the ankle replaced and hot bandages applied, and other repairs were made, which took up most of the afternoon.

When the doctor got through, he called Mrs. Bailey and myself out into the parlor, and said that we must not let people crowd in to see the patient; that his wounds were not dangerous, but very painful; that Miles was weak from loss of blood, and that his constitution was not in particularly good condition. The doctor, in fact, thought that Miles would be in great luck if he got out of the scrape without a run of fever. Thereafter Mrs. Bailey referred all visitors to me. I talked with the doctor and the nurse, and we all agreed that it would stop most inquisitive people to simply say that the patient had suffered an amputation.

That evening, when I went home, there were two anxious women to receive me, and the younger of them looked suspiciously as if she had been crying. I told them something of the accident, how it all happened, and about Miles's injuries. Both of them wanted to go right down and help "do something," but I told them of the doctor's order and of his fears.

By this time the reporters came; and I called them into the parlor, and then let them pump me. I detailed the accident in full, but declined to tell anything about Miles or his history. "The fact is," said I, "that you people won't give an engineer his just dues. Now, if Miles Diston had been a fireman and had climbed down a ladder with a child, you would have his picture in the paper and call him a hero and all that sort of thing; but here is a man crushed, bleeding, with broken bones, and a crippled engine, who stands on one foot, lashed to his reverse lever, for eighty miles, and making the fastest time ever made over the road, because he knew that others were suffering for the relief he brought."

"That's nerve," said one of the young men.

"Nerve!" said I, "nerve! Why, that man knows no more about fear than a lion; and think of the sand of the man! This afternoon he sat up and watched the doctor perform that amputation without a quiver; he wouldn't take chloroform; he wouldn't even lie down."

"Was the amputation above or below the knee?" asked the reporter.

"Below" (I didn't state how far).

"Which foot?"

"Left."

"He is in no great danger?"

"Yes, the doctor says he will be a very sick man for some time—if he recovers at all. Boys," I added, "there's one thing you might mention—and I think you ought to—and that is that it is such heroes as this that give a road its reputation; people feel as though they were safe behind such men."

If Miles Diston had read the papers the next morning he would have died of flattery; the reporters did themselves proud, and they made a whole column of the "iron will and nerves of steel" shown in that "amputation without ether."

Marie Venot was full of sympathy for Miles; she wanted to see him, but Mrs. Bailey referred her to me, and she finally went home, still inquiring every day about him. I don't think she had much other feeling for him than pity. She was down again a week later, and I talked freely of going to pick out a wooden foot for Miles, who was improving right along.

Meanwhile, the papers far and near copied the articles about the "Hero of the Throttle," and the item about the road's interest in heroes attracted the attention of our general passenger agent—he liked the free advertising and wanted more of it—so he called me in one day, and asked if I knew of a choice run they could give Miles as a reward of merit.

I told him, if he wanted to make a show of gratitude from the road, and get a big free advertisement in the papers, to have Miles appointed superintendent of the Spring Creek branch, where a practical man was needed, and then give it out "cold" that Miles had been rewarded by being made superintendent of the road. This was afterwards done, with a great hurrah (in the papers).

The second Sunday after Miles was hurt, Marie was down, and I thought I'd have a little fun with her, and see how she regarded Miles.

"There's quite a romance connected with Diston's affair," said I at the dinner table, rather carelessly. "There is a young lady visiting here in town—I hear she is very wealthy—who saw Miles when we took him off his engine. She sends flowers every day, calls him her hero, and is just crazy for him to get well so she can see him."

"Who is she, did you say?" asked my wife.

"I forgot her name," said I, "but I am here to tell you that she will get Miles if there is any chance in the world. Her father is an army officer, but she says that Miles Diston is a greater hero than the army ever produced."

"She's a hussy," said Marie.

I don't know whether you would call that

a bull or a bear movement on the Diston stock, but it went up—I could see that.

A week later Miles was able to come down to our house for dinner, and my wife asked Marie to come also. I met her at the depot, and after she was safe in the buggy, I told her that Miles was up at the house. She nearly jumped out; but I quieted her, and told her she mustn't notice or say a word about Miles's game leg, as he was extremely sensitive about it.

My wife was in the kitchen, and I went to the barn to put out the horse. Marie went to the sitting-room to avoid the parlor and Miles, but he was there, I guess, and Marie found her hero, for when they came out to dinner he had his arm around her. They were married a month later, and went to Washington, stopping to see us on the way back.

As I came home that night with my patent dinner pail, and with two rows of wrinkles and a load of responsibility on my brow, Marie shook her fist in my face and called me "an old story-teller."

"Story-teller," said I; "what story?"

"Oh, what story? That *leg* story, of course, you old cheat."

"What leg story?"

"Old innocence; that amputation below the knee—you know."

"Wa'n't it below the knee?"

"Yes, but it was only the little toe."

"John," said Miles, "she cried when she looked for that wooden foot and only found a slightly flat wheel."

"That's just like 'em," said I. "Here Marie only expected a part of a hero, and we give her a whole man, and she kicks—that's gratitude for you."

"I got my hero all right, though," said Marie; "you told me a big fib just the same, but I could kiss you for it."

"Don't you do that," said I; "but if the Lord should send you many blessings, and any of 'em are boys, you might name one after me."

She said she'd do it—and she did.

My Lady of the Eyes

MY LADY OF THE EYES

ONE morning, some years ago, I struck the general master mechanic of a Rocky Mountain road for a job as an engineer—I needed a job pretty badly.

As quick as the M. M. found that I could handle air on two hundred foot grades, he was as tickled as I was; engineers were not plenty in the country then, so many deserted to go to the mines.

"The 'III' will be out in a couple of days, and you can have her regular, unless Hopkins comes back," said he.

I hustled around for a room and made my peace with the boarding-house people before I reported to break in the big consolidation that was to fall to my care.

She was big and black and ugly and new, and her fresh fire made the asphalt paint on her fire-box and front-end stink in that peculiar and familiar way given to recently rebuilt engines; but it smelt better to me than all the perfumes of Arabia.

A good-natured engineer came out on the ash-pit track to welcome me to the West and the road, and incidentally to remark that it was a great relief to the gang that I had come as I did.

"Why," I asked, "are you so short-handed that you are doubling and trebling?" "No, but they are afraid that some of 'em will have to take out the 'III'—she is a holy terror."

Hadn't she been burned the first trip? Didn't she kill Jim O'Neil with the reverse lever? Hadn't she lain down on the bed of the Arkansas river and wallowed on "Scar Face" Hopkins, and he not up yet? Hadn't she run away time and again without cause or provocation?

But a fellow that has needed a job for six months will tackle almost anything, and I tackled the "holy terror."

In fixing up the cab, I noticed an extra bracket beside the steam gage for a clock,

"We carried him into the depot."
(page 88.)

and mentally noted that it would come in handy just as soon as I had a twenty dollar bill to spare for one of those jeweled, nickle-plated, side-winding clocks, that are the pride and comfort of those particular engineers who want nice things, with their names engraved on the case.

Before I had got everything ready to take the "three aces" over the turn-table for her breaking-in trip, the foreman of the back-shop came out with a package done up in a pair of old overalls, and said that here was Hopkins's clock, which I might as well use until he got around again—'fraid someone would steal it if left in his office.

Hopkins's clock was put on its old bracket.

Hopkins must have been one of those particular engineers; his clock was a fine one; "S. H. Hopkins" was engraved on the case in German text. The lower half of the dial was black with white figures, the upper half white with black figures. But what struck me was part of a woman's face burned into the enamel. Just half of this face showed, that on the white part of the dial; the black half hid the rest.

It was the face, or part of the face, of a handsome young woman with hair parted in the middle and waved back over the ears, a broad forehead, and such glorious eyes— eyes that looked straight into yours from every view point—honest eyes—reproving eyes—laughing eyes—loving eyes. I mentally named the picture "Her Eyes."

Now, I was not and am not sentimental or superstitious. I'd been married and helped wean a baby or two even then, but those eyes bothered me. They hunted mine and looked at me and asked me questions and made me forget things, and made me think and dream and speculate; all of which are sheer suicide for a locomotive engineer.

I got a switchman and started out to limber up the "III." I asked him to let me out on the main line, took a five-mile spin, and sidetracked for a freight train. While the man was unlocking the switch, I looked into the eyes and wondered what their owner was, or could be, or had been, to "Scar Faced"

Hopkins, and—ran off the switch. Then I wondered if Hopkins was looking into those eyes when he and the "III" went into the Arkansas river that dark night.

A few days after this the "III," Dennis Rafferty and I went into the regular freight service of the road.

On the first trip, when half way up Greenhall grade, I glanced at the clock and was startled. The "Eyes" were looking at me; there was a scared, pained look, a you-must-do-something look in the eyes, or it seemed to me there was.

"Damn that clock," said I to myself, "I'm getting superstitious or have softening of the brain," and I reached over to open the front door, so that the breeze could cool me off. In doing so my hand touched the water pipe to the injector—it was hot. The closed overflow injector was new to me; it had "broke," and was blowing steam back to the tank that I thought was putting water into the boiler. I put it to work properly and "felt of the water:" there was just a flutter in the lower gage cock; in five minutes the crown sheet and my reputation would have been burned beyond recognition. Those eyes were good for something after all.

I looked at them and they were calm. "It's all right now, but be careful," they said.

Dennis Rafferty had troubles of his own. The liner came off the new fire door letting the door get red hot, but it wasn't half as hot as Dennis. He hammered it with the coal pick and burned his hands and swore, and Dennis was an artist in profanity. He stepped up into the cab wiping his face on his sleeve, and ripping the English and profane languages into tatters; but he stopped short in the middle of an oath and looked ashamed, glanced at me, crossed himself and went back to his work quietly. When he came back into the cab, I asked him what choked him so sudden.

"Her," said he, nodding his head toward the clock. "Howly Mither, man, she looked hurted and sorry-like, same's me owld mither uster, whin I was noctious with the blasthfemry." So the "Eyes" were on Dennis, too. That took some of the conceit out of me, I was getting foolish about the eyes.

We had a time order against a passenger train, it would be sharp work to make the next station, the train was heavy, the road and the engine new to me, and I hesitated. The conductor was dubious but said the "204" or Frosty Keeler could do it any day of the week. I looked at my watch and then at the clock. The eyes looked "Yes, go, you can do it easily; the 'III' will do all you ask; trust her." I went, and as we pulled our caboose in to clear and before the express whistled for the junction, the eyes looked "Didn't I tell you; wasn't that splendid." Those eyes had been over the road more than I had, and knew the "III" better. I would trust the eyes.

On the return trip, a night run, I had a big train and a bad rail, but the "III" did splendid work and made her time while "Her Eyes" approved every move I made, smiled at me and admired my handling of the engine. The conductor unbent enough to send over word that it was the best run he'd ever had from a new man, but the "Eyes" looked, "That's nothing, you can do it every time, I know you can."

Half over the division, we took a siding for the "Cannon Ball." We cleared her ten minutes and I had time to oil around while Dennis cleaned his fire. I climbed up into the cab, wiping the long oiler and glanced at the clock. The "Eyes" were looking wild alarm—"do something quick." The "Eyes" had the look, or seemed to me to have the look, you might expect in those of a bound woman who sees a child at the stake just before the fire is lighted—immeasurable pain, pity, appeal. I tried the water, unconsciously; it was all right. I stepped into the gangway and glanced back. Our tail-lights were "in" and the white light of the switch flashed safely there, and we had backed in any way. I glanced ahead. The switch light was white, the target showed main line plainly, for my headlight shone on it full and clear. What could be the matter with "Her Eyes."

As I turned to enter the cab the roar of

the coming express came down the wind on the frosty air and my eyes fell on the rail ahead. My God, they were full to the siding! It was a stub-rail switch, and the stand had moved the target and the light, but not the rails—the bridle-rod was broken.

I yelled like a mad man, but the brakeman had gone to the caboose for his lunch pail. I ran to the switch. It was useless. I fought it an instant and then turned to the rails. Putting my foot against the main line rail, I grasped the switch rail and throwing all my strength into the effort, jerked it over to the main line, but would it stay until the train passed over? I felt sure it would not. I looked about for something to hold it. Part of a broken pin was the only thing in sight. The headlight of the express shone in my face, and something seemed to say, "This is your trial, do something quick." I threw myself prone on the ground, my head near the rails, and held the broken pin between the end of the siding rail and the main line. The switch rails could not be forced over without shearing off the pin. The corner of the pilot of the flying demon caught my right sleeve and tore it off, and the cloth threw the cylinder cocks open with a hiss, the wind and dust blinded and shook me, and the rails hammered and bruised and pinched my hand, but I held on. Twenty seconds later I sat watching the red lights of the tenth sleeper whip themselves out of sight. Then I went back to the cab, and "Her Eyes" glorified me. "God bless your dear eyes," said I, "where would we have all been now but for you?"

But the "Eyes" deprecated my remarks, and looked me upon a pedestal, but the company doctor dressed my hand the next day, and the superintendent gave the whole crew ten days for backing into that siding.

Another round trip, and I fear I watched "Her Eyes" more than the signals and the track ahead. "Her Eyes" decided for me, chose for me, approved and disapproved. I was running by "Her Eyes."

In a telegraph office they asked me if I could do something in a certain time and I was dazed. I didn't give my usual quick decision, my judgment was wobbly and uncertain. I must look at my clock—and "Her Eyes." I went out to the "III" to consult them, lost my chance and was "put in the hole" all over the division by the disgusted dispatcher.

Then I got to thinking and moralizing and sitting in judgment on my thraldom. Was I running the "III" or was "Her Eyes?" Did the company pay me for my knowledge, judgment, experience and skill in handling a locomotive, or for obeying orders from "Her Eyes." Any fool could obey orders.

Then I declared for liberty, but I kept away from "Her Eyes." I declared for liberty in the roundhouse.

I am a man of decision, and no sooner had I taken this oath than I got a screw driver, climbed into the cab of the "III," without looking at "Her Eyes," held my hand over the face of the clock and took it down. I wrapped it up and took it back to the foreman.

"Why, yes," said he, " 'Scar Face' was

here for it this morning. He's round somewhere yet. Ain't goin' to railroad no more, goin' into the real estate business. He's got money, so's his wife—daffool he didn't quit long ago."

"If 'Scar Face' Hopkins puts that clock over his desk and trusts 'Her Eyes,' he'll get rich," thought I. Perhaps, though, those eyes don't reach the soul of "Scar Face" Hopkins; perhaps he don't see them change as I did; men are conceited that way.

During the next month I got acquainted with "Scar Face" Hopkins, who was a first-class fellow, with a hand-clasp like a polar bear, a heart like a steam pulsometer, and a face that looked as if it might have been used for the butting post at the end of the world.

"Scar Face" Hopkins got all his scars in the battle of life. Men who command locomotives on the firing line often get hurt, but Hopkins had votes of thanks from officials and testimonials from men, and life-saver's medals from two governments to show that his scars were the brands of honorable degrees conferred by the Almighty on the field for brave and heroic deeds well done.

"Scar Face" Hopkins was a fellow you'd like to get up close to of a night and talk with, and smoke with, and think with, until unlawful hours.

One day I went into his office and the clock was there, and his old torch and a nickle-plated oiler, mementoes of the field. I looked at the clock, and "Her Eyes" smiled at me, or I thought they did, and said, just as plain as words, "Glad to see you, dear friend; sit down." But I turned my back to that clock; I can resist temptation when I know where it is coming from.

One day, a few weeks later, I stopped before a store window in a crowd to examine some pictures, satisfied my curiosity, and in stepping back to go away, put the heel of my number ten on a lady's foot with that peculiar "craunch" that you know hurts. I turned to make an apology, and faced the original of the picture on the clock. A beautiful pair of eyes, the rest of the face was hidden by a peculiar arrangement of veil that crossed the bridge of the nose and went around the ears and neck.

Those eyes, full of pain at first, changed instantly to frank forgiveness, and, bowing low, I repeated my plea for pardon for my clumsy carelessness, but was absolved so absolutely and completely, and dismissed so naturally, that I felt relieved.

I sauntered up to Hopkins' office. "Hopkins," said I, "I just met your wife."

"You did?"

"Yes, and I stepped on her foot and hurt her badly, I know." Then I told him about it.

"What did she say?" asked Hopkins, and I noticed a queer look. I thought it might be jealousy.

"Why, well, why I don't know as I remember, but it was very kindly and ladylike."

There was a queer expression on Hopkins' face.

"Of course—"

"Sure she spoke?" asked Hopkins. "How did you know it was my wife anyway?"

"Because it was the same face that is pictured on your clock, and some one in the crowd said it was Mrs. Hopkins. You know Hop., I ran by that clock for a few weeks, and I noticed the eyes."

"Anything queer about 'em?" This was a challenge.

"Yes, I think there is. In the first place, I know you will understand me when I say they are handsome eyes, and I'm free to confess that they had a queer influence on me, I imagined they changed and expressed things and—"

"Talked, eh."

"Well, yes." Then I told Hopkins the influence the "Eyes" had on me.

He listened intently, watching me; when I had finished, he came over, reached out his hand and said:

."Shake, friend, you're a damned good fellow."

I thought Hopkins had been drinking—or looking at "Her Eyes." He pulled up a chair and lit a cigar.

"John," said he, "it isn't every man that can understand what my wife says. Only kindred spirits can read the language of the eyes. *She hasn't spoken an audible word in ten years,* but she talks with her eyes, even her picture talks. We, rather she, is a mystery here; people believe all kinds of things about her and us; but we don't care. I want you to come up to the house some evening and know her better. We'll be three chums, I know it, but don't ask questions; you will know things later on."

Before I ever went to Hopkins' house, he had told her all about me, and when he introduced us, he said:

"Madeline, this is the friend who says your picture talked to him."

I bowed low to the lady and tried to put myself and her at ease.

"Mrs. Hopkins, I'm afraid your husband is poking fun at me, and thinks my liver is out of order, but, really, I did imagine I saw changing expression in your eyes in that picture—in fact, I named you 'My Lady of the Eyes.'"

She laughed—with her eyes—held out her hands and made me welcome.

"That name is something like mine," said Hopkins, "I call her 'Talking Eyes.'"

Then Hopkins brought in his little three-year-old daughter, who immediately climbed on my knee, captured my watch, and asked:

"What oo name?"

"John," said I.

"Don, Don," she repeated; "my name Maddie."

"That's Daddy's chum," put in Hopkins.

"Tum," repeated Maddie.

"Uncle Chummy," said Hopkins.

"Untle Tummie."

And I was "Untle Tummie" to little Madeline and "Chummy" to Hopkins and his wife from then on.

Mrs. Hopkins wore her veil at home as well as abroad, but it was so neatly arranged and worn so naturally that I soon became entirely used to it, in fact, didn't notice it. Otherwise, she was a well-dressed, handsomely set up woman, a splendid musician and a capital companion. She sat at her work listening, while Hopkins and I "railroaded" and argued about politics, and religion and everything else under the sun. Mrs. Hopkins took sides freely; a glance at her eyes told where she stood on any question.

Between "Scar Face" Hopkins and his handsome wife there appeared to be perfect sympathy and confidence. Sitting in silence, they glanced from one to the other now and again, smiled, nodded—and understood.

I was barred from the house for a month during the winter because little Madeline had the scarlet fever, then epidemic, but it was reported a light case and I contented myself with sending her toys and candy.

One day I dropped into Hopkins' office to make inquiry, when a clerk told me Hopkins had not been to the office for several days. Mrs. Hopkins was sick. I made another round trip and inquired again, and got the same answer; then I went up to the house.

The officious quarantine guard was still walking up and down in front of the Hopkins residence. To a single inquiry, this voluble functionary volunteered the information that the baby was all right now, but the lady herself was very sick with scarlet fever. Hopkins was most crazy, no trained nurses could be had for love nor money, the doctor was coming three times a day, and did I know that Mrs. Hopkins was some kind of a foreign Dago, and the whole outfit "queer?"

Hopkins was in trouble; I pushed open the gate and started up the walk.

"Hey, young feller, where yer goin'," demanded the guard.

"Into the house, of course."

"D'ye know if you go in ye got to stay for the next two weeks?"

"Perfectly."

"Then go on, you darned fool."

And I went on.

Hopkins met me, hollow-eyed and haggard.

"Chum," said he, "you've come to prison, but I'm glad. Help is out of reach. If you can take care of Maddie, the girl will do the cooking and I will—I will do my duty."

And night and day he did do his duty,

being alone with his wife except for the few moments of the doctor's calls.

One evening, after my little charge had been put to sleep downstairs by complying with her invariable order to "tell me a 'tory 'bout when oo was a 'ittle teenty weenty boy," the doctor came down with a grave face.

"Our patient has reached the worst stage —delirium. The turn will come to-night. Poor Hopkins is about worn out, and I'm afraid may need you. Please don't go to bed; be 'on call.' "

One hour, two hours, I sat there without hearing a sound from upstairs. I was drowsy and remembering that I had missed my evening smoke I lighted my pipe, silently opened the front door and stepped out upon the porch to get a whiff of fresh air. It was a still dark night, and I tiptoed down to the end that overlooked the city and stood looking at the lights and listening to the music of the switch engines in the yards below the hill. The porch was in darkness except the broad beam of light from the hall gas jet through the open door.

The lights below made me think of home and my wife and little ones sleeping safely, I hoped, close to the coastwise lights of the Old Colony.

I thought I heard a stealthy footfall behind me, and turned around to face an apparition that made the cold chill creep up my back. If ever there was a ghost, this must be one, an object in white not six feet from me.

I'm not at all afraid of ghosts when I reach my second wind, and I grabbed at this one. It moved backward silently and as I made a quick step toward it that specter let out the most blood-curdling yell I ever heard —the shriek of a maniac.

I stepped quicker now, but it moved away until it stood in the flood of light from the doorway, and then I saw a sight that took all the strength out of me. The most awful and frightful face I ever beheld, and,—it was the face of Madeline Hopkins.

The neck and jaw and mouth were drawn

and seamed and scarred in a frightful and hideous manner, the teeth protruded and the mouth was drawn to one side in a frightful leer; above that was all the beauty of "My Lady of the Eyes."

For a moment I was dumb and powerless, and in that moment Hopkins appeared with a bound, and between us we captured my poor friend's wife and struggled and fought with her up the long stairs and back to her bed.

Sitting one on either side, we had all we could do to hold her hands. She would lift us both to our feet, she was struggling desperately, and the eyes were the eyes of a tigress.

When this strain was at its worst and every nerve on edge, another scream from behind us cut our ears like a needle, the eyes of the tigress as well as ours sought the door, and there in her golden curls and white "nightie" stood little Madeline. The eyes of the tigress softened to tenderest love, and with a bound, the baby was on her mother's breast, her arms around her neck, and she was saying, "Poor Mama, what they doin' to poor Mama?"

"My darling, my darling," said the mother in the sweetest of tones.

I unconsciously released my hold upon the arm I held, and she drew the sheet up and covered her face as I was wont to see it, and held it there. With the other, she gently stroked the baby curls.

I watched this transformation as if under a spell.

Suddenly she turned her head toward Hopkins, her eyes full of tenderness and pity and love, reached out her hand and said:

"Oh, Steadman, my voice has come back, God has taken off the curse."

But poor Hopkins was on his knees beside the bed, his face buried in his arms, his strong shoulders heaving and pitiful sobs breaking from his very heart.

A couple of months afterward I resigned to go back to God's country, the home of the east wind, and where I could know my own children and speak to my own wife without an introduction, and the Hopkins invited me to a farewell dinner.

"My Lady of the Eyes" presided, looking handsomer and stronger than usual, but she didn't eat with us. But with eyes and voice she entertained us so royally and pleasantly that Hopkins and I did eating enough for all.

After supper, Hop. and I lighted our cigars and "railroaded" for awhile, then "Her Eyes" went to the piano and sang a dozen songs as only a trained singer can. Her voice was wonderfully sweet and low. They were old songs, but they seemed the better for that, and while she sang Hopkins's cigar went out and he just gazed at her with pride and joy in every lineament of his scarred and furrowed face.

Little Maddie was allowed to sit up in honor of "Untle Tummy," but after awhile the little head bobbed quietly and the little chin fell between the verses of her mother's song, and "My Lady of the Eyes" took her by the hand and brought her over to us.

"Tell papa good-night and Uncle Chum my good-bye, dear, and we'll go to bed."

Hopkins kissed the baby, and I got my hug, and another to take to my "ittle dirl," and Mrs. Hopkins held out both her hands to me.

"Good-bye, dear Chum," said she, "my love to you and yours, now and always."

Hopkins put his arm around his wife, kissed her forehead and said:

"Sweetheart, I'm going to tell Chum a story."

"And don't forget the hero," said she, and turning to me, "Don't believe all he says, and don't blame those that he blames, and remember that what is, is best, and seeming calamities are often blessings in disguise."

Hopkins and I looked into each other's faces and smoked in silence for ten minutes, then he turned to his secretary and, opening a drawer, took out a couple of cases and opened them. They contained medals. Then he opened a package of letters and selected one or two. We lighted fresh cigars and Hopkins began his story.

"My father was a pretty well-to-do business man and I his only child. My mother died when I was young. I managed to get through a grammar school and went to college. I wanted to go on the road from the time I could remember and had no ambition higher than to run a locomotive. That was my ideal of life.

"My father opposed this very strenuously, and offered to let me go to work if I'd select something decent—that's the way he put it. He used to say, 'Try a brick-yard, you might own one some day, you'll never own a railroad.' I had my choice, college or 'something decent,' and I took the college, although I didn't like it.

"The summer before I came of age my father died suddenly and my college life ended."

Here Hopkins fumbled around in his papers and selected one.

"Just to show you how odd my father was, here is the text of his will, leaving out the legal slush that lawyers always pack their papers in:

"'To my son, Steadman Hudson Hopkins, I leave one thousand dollars to be paid immediately on my demise. All the residue of my estate consisting of etc., etc.'—six figures, Chum, a snug little wad—'shall be placed in the hands of three trustees'—naming the presidents of three banks—'to be invested by them in state, municipal or government bonds, principal and interest accruing to be paid by said trustees to my son hereinbefore mentioned when he has pursued one calling, with average success, for ten consecutive years, and not until then. All in the best judgment of the trustees aforenamed.

"'To my son I also bequeath this fatherly advice, knowing the waste of money by heirs who have done nothing to produce it, and knowing that had I been given a fortune at the beginning of my career, it would have been lost for lack of business experience, and knowing too, the waste of time usually made by young men who drift from one employment or occupation to another—having wasted fifteen years of my own life in this way—I make these provisions in this my last will and testament, believing that in the end, if not now, my son will see the wisdom of this provision, etc., etc.'

"The governor had a long, clear head and he knew me and young men in general, but bless you, I thought he was a little mean at the time.

"I turned to the trustees and asked what they would consider as fulfilling the requirements of the will.

" 'Any honorable employment,' answered the oldest man of the trio.

"The next day, I went to see Andy Bridges, general superintendent of the old home road, who had been a friend of father's, and told him I wanted to go railroading. He offered to put me in his office, but I insisted on the foot-board, and to make a long story short, was firing inside of three weeks and running inside of three years.

"I was the proudest young prig that ever pulled a throttle. I always loved the work and—well, you know how the first five years of it absorbs you if you are cut out for it and like it and intend to stay at it.

"I had been running about two years, and had paid about as much attention to young women as I had to the subject of astronomy, until Madelene Bridges came out of a Southern convent to make her home with her uncle, our 'old man.'

"The first time I saw her I went clean, stark, raving, blind, drunken daft over her. I tried to argue and reason myself out of it, but it was no go. I didn't even know who she was then.

"But I was in love and, being so, wasn't hardly safe on the road.

"Then I spruced up and started in to see if I couldn't interest her in me half as much as I was interested in her.

"I didn't have much trouble to get a start, for Andy Bridges had come up from the ranks and hadn't forgotten it—most of 'em do—and welcomed any decent young man in his house, even if he was a car hand. Madelene had a couple of marriageable cousins then and that may account for old Andy.

"I got on pretty well at first, for I was first in the field. I got in a theatre or two before the other young fellows caught on. About this time there was a dance, and I lost my grip. I took Madelene but couldn't dance, and all the others could, especially Dandy Tamplin, one of the train despatchers.

"I took private dancing lessons, however, and squared myself that way.

"Singing was a favorite mode of passing the evenings with the young folks at the Bridges's home, and I cursed myself for being tuneless.

"It finally settled down to a race between Tamplin and myself, and each of us was doing his level best. I was so dead in earnest and so truly in love that I was no fit company for man or beast, and I'm afraid I was twice as awkward and dull in Madelene's presence as in any other place.

"Dandy Tamplin was a handsome young fellow, and a formidable rival, for he was always well-dressed, a good talker and more or less of a lady's man. Besides that, he was on the ground all the time and I had to be away two-thirds of the time on my runs.

"I came in one trip determined to know my fate that very evening—had my little piece all committed to memory.

"As I registered I heard one of the other despatchers, behind a partition, telling some one that he was going to work Dandy's trick until eleven o'clock, and then the two entered into a discussion of Dandy's quest of the 'old man's' niece, one of them remarking that all the opposition he had was Hopkins and that wasn't worth considering. I resolved to get to Bridges's ahead of Tamplin.

"But man—railroad man, anyway—proposes and the superintendent disposes. I met Bridges at the door.

" 'Hopkins,' said he, 'I want you to do me a personal favor.'

" 'Yes, sir.'

" 'I want you to double out in half an hour on some perishable freight that's coming in from the West; there isn't one available engine in. Will you do it?'

"'Yes,' I answered, slowly, showing my disappointment. 'But, Mr. Bridges, I was particularly anxious to go up to your house to-night; I intend to ask—'

"'I know, I know,' said he kindly, taking my hand; 'It'll be all right I hope; there ain't another young chap I'd like to see go up *and stay* better than you, but my son, *she will keep,* and this freight wont. You go out, and I'll promise that no one shall get a chance to ask ahead of you.' This was a friend at court and a strong one.

"'It means a lot to me,' said L

"'I know it my boy, and I'm proud to have you say so right out in meeting, but— well, you get those fruit cars in by moonlight, and I'll have you back light, and you can have the front parlor for a week.'

"On my return trip, I found a big Howe truss bridge on fire and didn't get in for two days. The road was blocked, everything out of gear and I had to double back again, whether or no.

"I was 'chewing the rag' with a roundhouse foreman about it when Old Andy came along.

" 'Go on, Hopkins,' said he, 'and you can lay off when you get brck. I'm going South with my car *and will take the girls with me!*'

"That was hint enough, and I said yes.

"It was in the evening, and while the fireman and I got our supper, the hostler turned my engine, coaled her up, took water and stood her on the north branch track, next the head end of her train, that had not yet been entirely made up.

"This north branch came into the south and west divisions off a very heavy grade and on a curve, the view being cut off at this point by buildings close to the track. The engine herself stood close to the office building, and after oiling around, I backed on to the train, bringing my cab right opposite a window in the despatcher's office. Just before this open window and facing me sat Dandy Tamplin at his key. I hated Dandy Tamplin.

"It was dark outside and in the cab, the conductor had given me my orders and said we'd go just as quick as the pony found a couple of cars more and put them on the hind end. Dennis had put in a big fire for the hill, and then gone skylarking around the station, and I was in the dark glaring at Dandy Tamplin in the light.

"The blow-off cock on this engine was on the right side and opened from the cab. Ordinarily, you pulled the handle up, but the last time the boiler was washed out they had turned the plug cock half over and the handle stuck up through the deck among the oil cans ahead of the reverse lever, and opened by pushing it down. I remember thinking it was dangerous, as a man might accidentally open it. On the cock was a piece of pipe to carry the hot water away from the paint work, and this stuck straight out under the footboard, the cock leaked a little and the end of the pipe dripped hot water and steam.

"While I glared at Tamplin, old man Bridges and the girls came into the room. Bridges went up to the narrow, shelf-like counter, looked at the register and asked Tamplin a question.

"Tamplin went up to the group, his back to me, and spoke to one after the other. Madelene was the last in the row and, while the others were talking, laid her gloves, veil and some flowers on the counter. Tamplin spoke to her and I could see the color change in her face. Oh! if I only had hold of Dandy Tamplin.

"Bridges hurried out into the hall behind the passage way, the girls following. Tamplin turned around and espied Madelene's belongings. He went up to them, smelled the flowers, then hurriedly took a note out of his pocket and slipped it into one of the gloves. The other glove he put in his breast pocket. It was well for Dandy Tamplin I didn't have a gun.

"Remember, all this happened quickly. Before Tamplin was fairly in his seat and at work, Madelene came tripping back alone and made for her bundle, but Tamplin left his key open and went over to her. I couldn't hear what was said for by this time the safety valves of my engine were blowing and drowned all sound. She evidently asked him what time it was and leaned partly over the counter to hear his reply. He put his hand under her chin and turned her face toward the clock, this with such an air of assurance that my heart sank—but murder was in my soul. Then quickly putting his hand behind her neck, he pulled her toward him and kissed her. I was a demon in an instant.

"She sprang away from him and ran into the hall and he came back to his chair with a smile of triumph on his thin lips.

"Somehow or other, just at this moment, I noticed the steam at the end of that blow-off pipe, and all the devils in hell whispered at once 'One move of your hand and your revenge is complete.' I wasn't Steadman Hopkins then, I was a madman bent on murder, and I reached down for that handle, holding on by the throttle with my left hand. The cock had some mud in it and I opened it wide before it blew out and then with a roar and a shriek it burst—and the crime was done.

"All the devils flew away at once and left

me alone, naked with my conscience. 'Murderer, murderer!' resounded in my ears; hisses, roars and screams seemed to come to fill my brain and dance around my condemned soul; voices seemed shrieking and crash upon crash seemed to smite my ears. I thought I was dying, and I remember distinctly how glad I was. I didn't let go of that valve, I couldn't—I'd go to hell with it in my hand and let them do their worst.

"Then remorse took possession of me. Wasn't it enough to maim and disfigure poor Tamplin, why cook him to death—I'd shut off that cock. I fought with it, but it wouldn't close, and I called Dennis to help me.

"Some one stood behind me and put a cool hand on my brow, and a woman's voice said, 'Poor brave fellow, he's still thinking of his duty; all the heroes don't live in books.'

"I opened my eyes, and looked around. I was in St. Mary's Hospital, and a nun was talking to herself.

"Well, John, I'd been there for more than six weeks, and it took six more before I understood just what had happened and could hobble around, for I had legs and ribs and an arm broken.

"It must have been at the moment I opened that blow-off cock that part of a runaway train came down the north grade, backward, like a whirlwind and buried my engine and myself, piling up an awful wreck that took fire. I was rescued at the last moment by the crowd of railroad men that collected and bodily tore the wreck apart to get at me. Every one thought I tried to close that blow-off cock and hold the throttle shut. I was a hero in the papers and to the men, and I couldn't get a chance to tell the truth if I dared, and I was afraid to ask about Dandy Tamplin.

"No word came from Madelene. One day Bridges came to see me, and brought me this watch I wear now, a present from the company. I determined to tell Bridges—but he wouldn't believe me. Looked, too, as if he thought I was off in my head yet and I must have looked crazy, for most of these brands I got that night. To be sure I've added to the collection here and there, but I never was pretty after that roundup.

"At last I mustered up courage and asked: 'How is Tamplin?' 'All right, working right along, but takes it hard,' said Bridges.

"'Was he laid up long? Is he as badly disfigured as I am?'

"'Why, man, he wasn't touched. He had gone to the other end of the room for a drink of water. I'm afraid, my boy, its Madelene he's worried about.'

"'She has refused him then?'

"'Well, I don't know that. She is still in bed, badly hurt. She has not seen a soul but her nurse, the doctor and my wife, and denies herself to all callers, even her best friends, even to me.'

"Chum, I won't tell you what I said or suffered. Madelene had come into the room again for her belongings, and had faced the dagger of steam sent by the hand of a man who would give his immortal soul to make her well again.

"I couldn't get around much, but I wrote

her a brief note asking if I might call and sent it by a messenger.

"She replied that she could not see me then. I waited. I hadn't the heart to write a confession I wanted to make in person, so after a week or two I went to the house.

"Madelene sent down word that she couldn't see me then and could not tell when she would see me.

"I thought the nurse, who acted as messenger, did not interpret either my message or hers as they were intended—I would write a note.

"I stepped into the library on one side of the hall, made myself at home and wrote Madelene a note, a love letter, begging for just one interview. Taking blame for all that had happened and confessing my love and devotion to her.

"It was a long letter and just as I finished it, I heard some one in the hall. I thought it was a servant and started for the doorway to ask her to carry my message. It was the nurse.

"I was partly concealed by the portieres.

She was facing the door, her finger on her lips, and before her stood Dandy Tamplin.

" 'It's all right' she whispered, 'be still,' and both of them tip-toed up-stairs.

"This, then was why I could not see Madelene. Dandy Tamplin was her accepted lover.

"That night I left the old home for good to seek my fortunes and forgetfulness far away. I didn't care where, so long as it was a great way off.

"At New York I found some engineers going out to run on the Meig's road in Peru. I signed a contract and in two days was on the Atlantic, bound for the Isthmus of Panama.

"I ran an engine in Peru until the war broke out with Chili. I was sent to the front with a train of soldiers one day and got on the battle field. Our side was getting badly worsted, and I got excited and jumping off the engine, armed myself and lit into the fight. A little crowd gathered around me and I found myself the leader, no officer in sight. There was a charge and we didn't run—surprised the Chilians. I got some of these blue brands on my left cheek there and made a new reputation. Before I knew it, I had on a uniform and dangled a sword. They nicknamed me the 'Fighting Yankee.'

"Peru had lots of trouble and I saw a good deal of it. When it was all over, I found myself in command of a gun boat, just a tug, but she was alive and had accounted for herself several times.

"The president sent me on a special mission to Chili just after the close of the war, and, all togged out in a new uniform, I went on board of an American ship at Callao bound for Valparaiso. I thought I was some pumpkins then. I'd lived a rough and tumble life for about three years and was beginning to like it—and to forget.

"I used to do the statuesque before the passengers, my scars attested my fighting propensities, and there were several Peruvian liars aboard that knew me by reputation, and enlarged on it.

"We touched at Coquimbo and an American civil engineer and family came aboard, homeward bound.

"That afternoon I was lolling in the smoking-room on deck, when I was attracted by the sound of ladies talking on the promenade just outside the open port where I sat. It was the engineer's wife and daughter.

" 'Mamma,' said the young lady. 'I must read you Madelene's letter. Poor, dear Madelene, it's just too sorrowful and romantic for anything.'

"Madelene! I hadn't heard that name pronounced for three years. It was wrong, I knew it, but I listened.

" 'Poor dear, she was awfully hurt and disfigured in a railroad wreck.'

"It was *my* Madelene they were talking about. Wild horses could not have dragged me from the spot.

"The girl read something like this. I know for I've read that letter a hundred times. It's in this pile here.

" 'Dear Lottie: Your ever welcome'— 'no, not that.'

" 'Uncle Andrew is going'—'let me see,

Oh! yes, here it is, now listen Mamma,' said the girl.

"'Dear Schoolmate. I have never told a soul about my troubles or my trials, for long I could not bear to think of them myself. But lately I have seen it in its true light, and have come to the conclusion that I have no right to moan my life away. I'm past all that, there is nothing for me to live for in myself, but my life is spared for some purpose, and I propose to devote it to doing good to others'—'isn't she a sweet soul, mamma?'

"'After I came to live with Uncle Andrew, I was very happy, it seemed like a release from prison. I saw much company, and in six months had two lovers—more than I deserved. One of these was a plain, honest manly man; he was one of Uncle Andrew's engineers. He wasn't handsome, but he was the kind of man that sensible women love. The other was a handsome, showy, witty man, also an employee of the railroad, considered 'the catch' among the girls. Really, Lottie, both of them tried to propose and I wouldn't let them, I didn't know which one of them I liked best. But if things had taken the usual course, I should have married the handsome one—and been sorry forever after.'

"My heart stood still—she hadn't married Dandy Tamplin after all."

" 'The night of the wreck, I was going out on Uncle Andrew's private car. The handsome man was on duty in the office. The plain man on an engine that stood before the open window, I didn't know that then.

' "A runaway train crashed into the engine and something exploded and a stream of boiling water came into the room and scalded me beyond recognition. You would not know me, Lottie, I am so disfigured.

" 'The handsome man did nothing but wring his hands; the plain one staid on the engine and tried to stop the steam from coming out, and was himself terribly injured.

" 'I was for weeks in bed and suffered mental agony much beyond the merely physical pain. I was so wicked I cursed my life and my Maker and prayed for death —yet I lived. I was so resentful, so heartbroken, so wicked, that I refused to speak for weeks, then, when I tried, I couldn't, God had put the curse of silence on my wickedness.'

"Think of Madelene being wicked, Chum.

" 'When I was getting well enough and reconciled to my own fate, enough to think of others, I thought of my two lovers. Then I asked my nurse for a glass. One look, and I made up my mind never to see either of them again.

" 'Both of them were clamoring to see me, and I refused to see either. The plain man wrote me the only love letter I ever received. I have worn it out reading it. It was so manly, so unselfish! He blamed himself for the accident, and offered me his devotion and love, no matter in what condition the letter found me. This letter he wrote in Uncle Andrew's library, left it open on the desk and—disappeared.

" 'I have never heard from him from that

day to this. I never could understand it. A man that could write that letter, couldn't run away. The last sentence in his letter proved that. It said: "Remember, dear Madelene, that somewhere, somehow, I am thinking of you always; that whether you see me or not, you will some day come to know that I love your soul, not your face; that your life is dear to me, and no calamity can make any difference."

" 'Those were brave words, and after I read them, I knew for the first time that this was the man I loved. They told me he was frightfully disfigured, too, but that made no difference to me, I loved him. But he was gone, no one knew where. Why did he go?

" 'The handsome man disappeared the same day, and he never came back, but he left no letter.

" 'Dear Lottie, I have only now solved the mystery. My sometime nurse has just confessed that the night the letter was written the other man came to the house, like a thief, he had bribed her to give me drugs to make me sleep and then she led him into my room and showed him my scars. If he ever loved me at all, he was in love with my face; the other man loved me. One went away because he saw me, the other one because he saw his rival apparently granted the interview refused to him. My true lover must have seen that man sneaking up to my room.'

"John, every fibre of my being danced for joy. I didn't hear the rest, and she read several pages. I had heard enough.

"I went right out on the deck, begged pardon to begin with, introduced myself, confessed to eavesdropping, told who I was, where I had been and asked for that letter.

"I got it and Madelene's picture; the one you have seen on my clock.

"I finished my task at Valparaiso while the vessel lay there, reported by mail, and came home on the same ship.

"I took that letter and photograph to Andy Bridges's house and wrote across the envelope 'Madelene Bridges, I demand your immediate and unconditional surrender, signed, Steadman H. Hopkins.'

"And I got it in five minutes. Chum, that

is the only case on record where something worth having was ever surrendered to an officer of the Peruvian government.

"In six months I was back on an engine in a new country, with my silent, loved and loving wife, in a new home. Three times before now someone has seen Madelene's face, twice I told this story, and then we moved away; once I told it and trusted, and it was not repeated. Madelene can stand being a mystery and wondered at, but she cannot stand pity and curiosity. As for you, old Chum, I haven't even asked you not to repeat what I have told you—I know you won't."

After a long while, I turned to Hopkins and said: "And yet, Hopkins, fools say there is no romance in railroad life. This is a story worth reading, and some day I'd like to write it."

"Not in Madelene's time, or in mine, Chum, but if ever a time comes, I'll send you a token."

"Send me your picture, Hop."

"No, I'll send you Madelene's. No, I'll

send you the clock with the 'talking eyes.'"

And standing at Hopkins's gate, the scarfaced man with the romance and I parted, like ships that meet, hail and pass on, never to meet again. Hopkins and I moved away from one another, each on his own course, across the seven seas of life.

And all this happened almost twenty years ago.

The other day, my office boy brought me a card that read, "Mrs. Henry Adams, Washington, D. C." "Is she a book agent?" I asked.

"Nope, don't look like one."

"Show her in."

A young woman came in, looked at me hard for a moment, laid a package on my desk and asked,

"Is this the Mr. Alexander who used to be an engineer?"

I confessed.

"I don't suppose you remember me," she asked.

I put on my glasses and looked at her. No, I never—then she put her handkerchief up to her lips covering the lower part of her face; it was the face of Madelene Hopkins.

"Yes," said I, "I remember you perfectly, seventeen or eighteen years ago you used to sit on my knee and call me 'Untle Tummy,' and I called you Maddie."

Then we laughed and shook hands.

"Mr. Alexander," said she, "In looking over some of father's papers, we came across a request that under certain conditions you were to be sent an old keepsake of his, a clock with mother's picture on it. I have brought it to you."

"And your father and mother, what of them, my friend?" I asked, for the promise of that clock "under certain conditions" was coming back to me.

"Haven't you heard, sir, poor papa and mama were lost in that awful wreck at Castleton, two years ago."

And as I write, from the dial of "Scar Faced" Hopkins's clock "My Lady of the Eyes" looks down at me from across the mystery of eternity. The eyes do not change as once they did, or has age dimmed my sight and imagination? Long I look into their peaceful depths thinking of their story, and ask, "Dear Eyes, is it well with thee?" —and they seem to answer, "It is well."

Some Freaks of Fate

SOME FREAKS OF FATE

I AM just back from a visit to old scenes, old chums and old memories of my interesting experience on the western fringe of Uncle Sam's great, gray blanket—the plains.

If some of these fellows who know more about writing than about running engines would only go out there for a year and keep their eyes and ears and brains open, and mouths shut, they could come home and write us some true stories that would make fiction-grinders exceedingly weary.

The frontier attracts strong characters, men with pioneer spirit, men who are willing to sacrifice something, in order to gain an end; men with loves and men with hates. Bad men are there, some of them hunted from Eastern communities, perhaps, but you will find no fools and mighty few weak faces

—there's character in every feature you look at.

Every one is there for a purpose; to accomplish something; to get ahead in the world; to make a new start; perhaps to live down something, or to get out of the rut cut by ancestors; some may only want to drink, and shout, and shoot, but even these do it with a vim—they mean it.

Of the many men who ran engines at the front, with me in the old days, I recall few whose lives were purposeless; almost every one had a life-story.

If there's anything that I enjoy, it's to sit down to a pipe and a life-story—told by the subject himself. How many have I listened to, out there, and every one of them worthy the pen of a Kipling!

The population of the frontier is never all made up of men, and the women all have strong features, too—self-sacrifice, devotion, degradation, or *something,* is written on every face. There are no blanks in that lottery—there's little material there for homes of feeble-minded.

It isn't strange, either, when you come to think of it; fools never go anywhere, they are just born and raised. If they move it's because they are "took"—you never heard of a pioneer fool.

One of the strongest characters I ever knew was a runner out there by the name of Gunderson—Oscar Gunderson. He was of Swedish parentage, very light-complexioned, very large, and a splendid mechanic, as Swedes are apt to be when they try. Gunderson's name was, I suppose, properly entered on the company's time-book, but it never was in the nomenclature of the road. With the railroaders' gift for abbreviation and nickname, Gunderson soon came down to "Gun," his size, head, hand or heart furnished the prefix of "Big," and "Big Gun" he remains to-day. "Big Gun" among his friends, but simple "Gun" to me. I think I called him "Gun" from the start.

Gun ran himself as he did his engine, exercised the same care of himself, and always talked engine about his own anatomy, clothes, food and drink.

His hat was always referred to as his "dome-casing;" his Brotherhood pin was his "number-plate;" his coat was "the jacket;" his legs the "drivers;" his hands "the pins;" arms were "side-rods;" stomach "firebox;" and his mouth "the pop."

He invariably referred to a missing suspender-button as a broken "spring-hanger;" to a limp as a "flat-wheel;" he "fired up" when eating; he "took water," the same as the engine; and "oiled round," when he tasted whisky.

Gun knew all the slang and shop-talk of the road, and used it—was even accused of inventing much of it—but his engine talk was unique and inimitable.

We roomed together a whole winter; and often, after I had gone to bed, Gun would come in, and as he peeled off his clothes he would deliver himself something as follows:

"Say, John, you don't know who I met on the up trip? Well, sir, Dock Taggert. I was sailin' along up the main line near Bob's, and who should I see but Dock backed in on the sidin'—seemed kinder dilapidated, like he was runnin' on one side. I jest slammed on the wind and went over and shook. Dock looks pretty tough, John—must have been out surfacing track, ain't been wiped in Lord knows when, oiled a good deal, but nary a wipe, jacket rusted and streaked, tire double flanged, valves blowin', packing down, don't seem to steam, maybe's had poor coal, or is all limed up. He's got to go through the back shop 'efore the old man'll ever let him into the roundhouse. I set his packin' out and put him in a stall at the Gray's corral; hope he'll brace up. Dock's a mighty good workin' scrap, if you could only get him to carryin' his water right; if he'd come down to three gauges he'd be a dandy, but this tryin' to run first section with a flutter in the stack all the time is no good—he must 'a flagged in."

Which, being translated into English, would carry the information that Gun had seen one of the old ex-engineers at Bob Slattery's saloon, had stopped and greeted him. Dock looked as if he had tramped, had drank, was dirty, coat had holes, soles of his boots badly worn, wheezing, seemed hungry and lifeless, been eating poor food, and was in a general run-down condition. Gun had "set out his packing" by feeding him and put him in a bed at the Grand Central Hotel—nicknamed the "Grayback's Corral." Gun thought he would have to reform, before the M. M. put him into active service. He was a good engineer, but drank too much, and lastly, he was in so bad a condition he could not get himself into headquarters unless someone helped him by "flagging" for him.

Gun was a bachelor; he came to us from the Pacific side, and told me once that he first went west on account of a woman, but —begging Mr. Kipling's pardon—that's another story.

"I don't think I'd care to double-crew my mill," Gun would say when the conversation turned to matrimony. "I've been raised to keep your own engine and take care of it, and pull what you could. In double-heading there's always a row as to who ought to go ahead and enjoy the scenery or stay behind and eat cinders."

I knew from the first that Gun had a story to tell, if he'd only give it up, and I fear I often led up to it, with the hope that he would tell it to me—but he never did.

My big friend sent a sum of money away every month, I supposed to some relative, until one day I picked up from the floor a folded paper dirty from having been carried long in Gun's pocket, and found a receipt. It read:

"MISSION, SAN ANTONIO, *Jan. 1, 1878.*
"Received of O. Gunderson, for Mabel Rogers, $40.00.
"SISTER THERESA."

Ah, a little girl in the story! I thought; it's a sad story, then. There's nothing so pure and beautiful and sweet and joyous as a little girl, yet when a little girl has a story it's almost always a sad story.

I gave Gun the paper; he thanked me; said he must look out better for those receipts, and added that he was educating a bit of a girl out on the coast.

"Yours, Gun?" I asked kindly.

"No, John; she ain't; I'd give $5,000 if she was."

He looked at me straight, with that clear, blue eye, and I knew he told me the truth.

"How old is she?" I asked.

"I don't know; 'bout five or six."

"Ever seen her?"

"No."

"Where did you get her?"

"Ain't had her."

"Tell me about her?"

"She was willed to me, John, kinder put in extra, but I can't tell you her story now, partly because I don't know it all myself, and partly because I won't—I won't even tell her."

I did not again refer to Gun's little girl, and soon other experiences and other biographies crowded the story out of my mind.

One evening in the spring, I sat by the open window, enjoying the cool night breeze from off the mountains, when I heard Gun's cheery voice on the porch below. He was lecturing his fireman, in his own, unique way.

"Well, Jim, if I ain't ashamed of you! There ain't no one but you; coming into general headquarters with a flutter in the stack, so full that you can't whistle, air-pump a-squealing 'count of water, smeared from stack to man-hole, headlight smoked and glimmery, don't know your own rights, kind o' runnin' wildcat, without proper signals, imagining you're first section with a regardless order. You want to blow out, man, and trim up, get your packing set out and carry less juice. You're worse than one of them slippin', dancin', three-legged, no-good Grants. The next time I catch you at hightide, I'll scrap you, that's what I'll do, fire you into the scrap-pile. Why can't you use some judgment in your runnin'? Why can't you say, 'Why, here's the town of Whisky, I'm going to stop here and oil around,' sail right into town, put the air on steady and fine, bring her right down to the proper gait, throw her into full release, so as to just stop right, shut off your squirt, drop a little oil on the worst points, ring your bell and sail on.

"But you, you come into town forty miles an hour, jam on the emergency and while the passengers pick 'emselves out of the ends of the cars, you go into the supply house and leave the injector on, and then, when you do move, you're too full to go without opening your cylinder cocks and givin' yourself dead away.

"Now, I'm goin' to Californ', next month, and if you get so as you can tell when you've got enough liquor without waiting for it to break your injectors, I'll ask the old man to let you finger the plug on Old Baldy whilst I'm gone. But I'm damned if I don't feel as if you was like that measly old 19—jest fit to be jacked up to saw wood with."

While Gun was in California, I was taken home on a requisition from my wife, and Oscar Gunderson and his little girl became a memory—a page in a book that I had partly read and lost, but not entirely forgotten.

One day last summer I took the westbound express at Topeka, and spreading my grip, hat, coat and umbrella, out on the seats, so as to resemble an experienced English tourist, I fished up a Wheeling stogie and a book and went into the smoking-pen of the sleeper, which I had all to myself for half-an-hour.

The train stopped to give the thirsty tender a drink and a man came in to wash his hands. He had been riding on the engine.

After washing, he stepped to the door of the "smokery,"struck a match on the leg of his pants, held both hands around the end of his cigar while he lighted it, then waving the match to put it out, he threw it down and came in.

While he was absorbed in all this, I took a glance at him. Six-foot-four, if an inch; high cheek bones; yellow beard; clear, blue eyes; white skin, and a hand about the size of a Cincinnati ham. I knew that face despite twelve years of turkey-tracks about the eyes.

"Gunderson, old man, how are you?" I said, offering my fin.

"Well, John Alexander, how in the name of thunder did you get away out here on the main stem, without orders?"

"Inspection-car," said I; "how did you get here?"

"Deadheading home; been out on special, a gilt-edged special, took her clean through to New York."

"You did!" I exclaimed; "why, how was that?"

"Went up special to a weddin', don't you see? Went up to see a new compound start off—prettiest sight I ever saw—working smooth as grease; but I'm kind of dubious about repairs and general running. I'm anxious to see how the performance sheet looks at the end of the year, John."

"Who's been double-heading, Gun?"

"Why—why, my little girl, trimmest, neatest, slickest little mill you ever saw. Lord! but she was painted red and white and gold-leaf, three brass bands on her stack, solid nickel trimming, all the latest improvements, corrugated firebox, high pressure smoke consumer and sand-jet—jest made a purpose for specials, and pay-car. But if she ain't got herself coupled onto a long-fire-boxed ten-wheeler, with a big lap and a Joy gear, you can put me down for a clinker. Yes, sir; the baby is a heart-breaker on dress-parade, and the ten-wheeler is a whale on business, and if they don't jump the track, you watch out for some express speed that will make the canals sick, see if they don't."

Without giving me time to say a word, he was off again.

"You ought to seen 'em start out, nary a slip, cutting off square as a die, small one ahead speaking her little piece chipper and fast on account of her smaller wheels, and the ten-wheeler barking bass, steady as a clock, with a hundred-and-enough on the gauge, a full throttle, and half a pipe of sand. You couldn't tell to save you whether the little one was pulling the big one or the big one shoving the little—never saw a relief train start out in such shape in my life."

Gunderson was evidently enthusiastic over the marriage of his little girl.

We talked over old times and the changes, and followed each other up to date with a great deal of mutual enjoyment, until the porter demanded the "smokery" for his bunk.

As we started for bed, Gun laid his hand on my shoulder and said:

"John, a good many years ago, you asked me to tell you the story of my little girl. I refused then for her sake. I'll tell you in the morning."

After a hearty breakfast and a good cigar, Gunderson squared himself for the story. He shut his eyes for a few minutes, as if to recall something, and then, speaking as if to himself, he said:

"Well, sir, there wasn't a simmer anywhere, dampers all shut; you wouldn't'a suspected they was up to the popping point, but the minute they got their orders, and the con. put up his hand, so, up went—"

"Say," I interrupted, "I thought I was to have the story. I believe you told me about the wedding, last night. The young couple started out well."

"Oh, yes, old man, I forgot, the story; well, get on the next pit here," motioning to a seat next to him, "and I'll give you the history of an old, hook-motion, name of Oscar Gunderson, and a trim, Class "G" made of solid silver, from pilot to draft-gear.

"You think I'm a Swede; well, I ain't, I don't know what I am, but I guess I come nearer to being a Chinaman than anything else. My father was a sea-captain, and my mother found me on the China sea—but they were both Swedes just the same. I had two sisters older than myself, and in order to better our chances, father moved to New York when I was less than five years old.

"He soon secured work as captain on a steamer in the Cuban trade, and died at sea, when I was ten.

"I had a bent for machinery, and tried the old machine-shops of the Central road, but soon found myself firing.

"I went to California, shortly after the war, on account of a woman—mostly my fault.

"Well, after running around there for some years, I struck a job on the Virginia & Truckee, in '73.

"Virginia City and Carson and all the Nevada towns were doing a fall-rush business, turning every wheel they had, with three crews to a mill. Why, if you'd go down street in any one of them towns at night, and see the crowds around the gamblers and molls, you'd think hell was a-coming forty-mile an hour, and that it wan't more than a car-length away.

"Well, one morning, I came into Virginia about breakfast time, and with the rest of the crew, went up to the old California Chop-house for breakfast. This same chop-house was a building about good-enough for a stable, these days; but it had a reputation then for steaks. All the gamblers ate there; and it's a safe rule to eat where the gamblers do, in a frontier town, if you want the best there is, regardless of price.

"It was early for the regular trade, and we had the dining-room mostly to ourselves, for a few minutes, then there were four women folks came in and sat down at a table bearing a card: 'Reserved for Ladies.'

"Three of them were dressed loud, had signs out whereby any one could tell that they wouldn't be received into no Four Hundred; but one of them was a nice-looking, modestly-dressed woman, had on half-mourning, if I remember. She had one of them sweet, strong faces, John, like the nun when I had my arm broke and was scalded, —her sweet mouth kept mumblin' prayers, but her fingers held an artery shut that was trying its damndest to pump Gun Gunderson's old heart dry—strong character, you bet.

"Well, that woman sat facing our table and kept looking at me; I couldn't see her without turning, but I knew she was looking. John, did you ever notice that you could *feel* the presence of some people; you knew they were near you without seeing them? Well, when that happens, don't forget to give that fellow due credit; for whoever it is he or she has the strongest mind—the dominant one.

"I *had* to look around at that woman. I shall never forget how she looked; her hand was on the side of her face; her great, brown, tender eyes were staring right at me—she was reading my very soul. I let her read.

"I had been jacking up a gilly of a gafter who had referred to his mother as "the old woman," and I didn't let the four females disturb me. I meant to hold up a looking glass for that young whelp to look into. I hate a man that don't love his mother.

"Why," says I, "you miserable example of Divine carelessness, do you know what that 'old woman' mother has done for you, you drivelin' idiot, a-thankin' God that you're alive and forgetting the very mother that bore you; if you could see the tears that she has shed, if you could count the sleepless nights that she has put in, the heartaches, the pain, the privation that she has humbly, silently, even thankfully borne that you might simply live, you'd squander your last cent and your last breath to make her life a joy, from this day until her light goes out. A man that don't respect his mother is lost to all decency; a man who will hear her name belittled is a Judas, and a man who will call his mother 'old woman' is a no-good, low-down, misbehaven whelp. Why, damn it, I'd fight a buzz-saw, if it called my mother 'old woman'—and she's been dead a long time; gone to that special, exalted, gilt-edged and glorious heaven for mothers. No one but mothers have a right to expect to go to a heaven, and the only question that'll be asked is, 'Have you been a mother?'

"Well, sir, I had forgot about the women, but they clapped their hands and I looked around, and there were tears in the eyes of that one woman.

"She got up; came to our table and laid a card by my plate, and said, 'I beg your pardon; but won't you call on me? Please do.'

"I was completely knocked out, but told her I would, and she went out alone; the others finished their breakfast.

"She had no sooner gone than Cy Nash, my conductor, commenced to giggle—'Made a mash on the flyest woman in town,' he tittered; 'ain't a blood in town but what would give his head for your boots, old man; that's Mabel Verne—owns the Odeon dance hall, and the Tontine, in Carson.'

"I glanced at the card, and it did read. 'Mabel Verne, 21 Flood avenue.'

"Well, Flood avenue is no slouch of a street, the best folks live there," I answered.

" 'Yes, that's her private residence, and if you go there and are let in, you'd be the first man ever seen around there. She's a curious critter, never rides or drives, or shows herself off at all; but you bet she sees that the rest of the stock show off. She's in it for money, I tell you.'

"I don't know why, but it made me kind of heart-sick to think of the hell that woman must be in, for I knew by her looks that she had a heart and a brain, and that neither of them was in the Odeon or the Tontine dance-houses.

"I thought the matter over,—and didn't go to see her. The next trip, she sent a carriage for me.

"She met me at the door, and took my hat, and as I dropped into an easy chair, I opened the ball to the effect that 'this here was a strange proceeding for a lady.'

" 'Yes,' said she, sitting down square in front of me; 'it is; I felt as if I had found a true man, when I first saw you, and I have asked you here to tell you a story, my story, and ask your help and advice. I am so earnest, so anxious to do thoroughly what I have undertaken, that I fear to overdo it; I need counsel, restraint; I can trust you. Won't you help me?"

" 'If I can; what is it that you want me to do, madam?'

" 'First of all, keep a secret, and next, protect or help protect, an innocent child.'

" 'Suppose I help the child, and you don't tell me the secret?'

" 'No, it concerns the child, sir; she is my child; I want her to grow up without knowing what her mother has done, or how she has lived and suffered; you wouldn't tell her that, would you?'

" 'No; certainly not!'

" 'Nor anyone else?'

" 'No.'

" 'You would judge her alone, forgetting her mother?'

" 'Yes.'

" 'Then I will tell you the story.'

"She got up and changed the window

blinds, so that the light shone on my face; I guess she wanted to study the effect of her words.

"'I was born at Sacramento,' she began; 'my father was a well-to-do mechanic, and I his only child; I grew up pretty fair-looking, and my parents spent about all they could make to complete my education, especially in music, of which I was fond. When I was eighteen years old, I fell in love with a young man, the son of one of the rich merchants of San Francisco, where we had removed. Like many another foolish girl, I trusted too implicitly, and believed too easily, and soon found myself in a humiliating position, but trusted to the honor of my lover to stand by me.

"'When I explained matters to him he seemed pleased, said he could fix that easy enough; we would get married at once and claim a secret marriage for some months past.

"'He arranged that I should meet him the next evening, and go to an old priest in an obscure parish, and be married.

"'I stood long hours on a corner, half dead with fear, that night, for a lover that never came. He's dead now, got run over in Oakland yard, that very night, as he was running away from me, and as I waited and shivered under the stars and the fire of my own conscience.'

"'Did he stand on one track, to get out of the way of another train, and get struck?' I asked.

"'Yes,' looking at me close.

"'Did he have on a false moustache, and a good deal of money and securities in a satchel, and everybody think at first he was a burglar?'

"'Yes; but how did you know that?'

"'Because, I killed him.'

"'You?'

"'Yes; I ran an engine over him, couldn't make him hear or see me. He was the first man I ever killed; strange he should be *this* particular man.'

"'It's fate,' said the woman, rocking slowly back and forth, 'it's fate, but it seems as though I like you better now that you were my avenger. That accident drove revenge out of my heart, caused me to let *him* be forgotten, and to live for my child. I have lived for her. I live to-day for her and I will continue to live for her.'

" 'My disgrace killed my mother and ruined my father. I swore I would be an honest woman, and I sought employment to earn a living for my babe and myself, but every avenue was closed to me. I washed and scrubbed while I was able to teach music splendidly, but I could get no pupils. I made shirts for a pittance and daily refused, to me, fortunes for dishonor. I have gone hungry and almost naked to pay for my baby's board, but I was hunted down at last.

" 'One day, after many rebuffs in seeking employment, I went to the home of a sister of my child's father, and took the baby, told her who I was and asked her to help me to a chance to work. The good woman scarcely looked at me or the child; she said that had it not been for such as I, poor Charles would have been alive; his blood was on my head; I ought to ask God to wash my blood-stained hands.

"'I went away from that house with my mind made up what to do. I would put my child in honest hands, and chain myself to the stake to suffer everlasting damnation for her sweet sake.

"'She is in the Mission San Antonio now, between three and four, a perfect little princess, she looks like me, and grows, oh, so lovely! If you could see her, you'd love her.

"'I can't go to see her any more; she is old enough to remember. The last time I was there, she demanded a papa!

"'I am making a great deal of money. Many of the rich men, whose Puritan wives and daughters refused me honest work, are squandering lots of their wealth in my houses. I am saving money, too; and propose, as soon as I can get a neat fortune together to go away to the ends of the earth, and have my little girl with me. I will raise her to know herself and to know mankind.'

" 'And what do you want me to do, madam?'

" 'I want you to be that child's guardian; the honest man through whom she will reach the outside of San Antonio and the world. Who will go between her and me until a happier time.'

" 'I am only a rough engineer; the child will be raised to consider herself well off, perhaps rich.'.

" 'Adopt her. I will stay in the background; make her expenditures and her education what you like. I will trust you.'

" 'I can't do that.'

" 'You are single; your life is hard; I have money enough for us all. Let us go to the Sandwich islands, anywhere, and commence life anew. The little one will know no other father, and all inquiry will be stopped.'

" 'I couldn't think of it, my dear madam; it's too easy; it's like pulling jerkwater passenger—I like through freight.'

"Well, John, to make a long story short, the interview ended about here, and several more got to about the same place. There were a thousand things I could not help but admire in that woman, and I liked her better the more I knew her. But it wan't love; it was a sort of an admiration for her love of the child, and the nerve she displayed in its behalf. But I shrank from becoming her husband or companion, although I think she loved me, in the end, better than she ever did anybody.

"However, I finally agreed to look after the little one, in case anything happened to the mother, and commenced then to send the money for her board and tuition, and the mother dropped out of all connection with the child or those having her in charge.

"The mother made her pile and got out of the business, and at my suggestion went down near Los Angeles and bought a nice country place, to start respectable before she took the little one home. She left money in Carson, subject to my check, for the little girl, and things slid along for a year or so all smooth enough.

"I was out on a snow-bucking expedition

one time the next winter, sleeping in cars, shanties or on the engine, and I soon found myself all bunged up with the worst dose of rheumatiz' you ever see. I had to get down to a lower altitude, and made for Sacramento in the spring. I paid the Mission a year in advance, and with less than a hundred dollars of my own, struck out, hoping to dodge the twists that were in my bones.

"A hundred blind gaskets don't go far when you're sick, and the first thing I knew I was dead broke; couldn't pay my board, couldn't buy medicine, couldn't walk—nothing but think and suffer. I finally had to go to a hospital. Not one of the old gang ever came to see me. Old Gun was a dandy, when he was making—and spending—a couple hundred a month; the rest of the time he was supposed to be dead.

"I might have died in the hospital, if fate hadn't decreed to send me relief. It suddenly dawned upon me that I was getting far better treatment than usual, had a special nurse, the best of food, flowers, etc., all labeled 'From the Boys.'"

"I found out, after I was well enough to take a sun bath on the porch, that a woman had sent all my luxuries, and that her purse had been opened for my relief. I knew who it was at once, and was anxious to get well and at work, so as not to live on one who was only too glad to do everything for me.

"A six months' wrastle with the twisters leaves a fellow stiff-jointed and oldish, and lying in bed takes the strength out of him. I took the notion to get out and go to work, one day, and walked down to the shops—I was carried back, chuck full of 'em again.

"The doctor said I must go to Ojo Caliente, away down south, if I was to get well. John, if the Santa Fé road had 'a been for sale for a cent then, I couldn't 'a bought a spike.

"At about the height of my ill-luck, I got a letter from Mabel Verne—she had another name, but that don't matter—and she asked me again to come to her; to have a home, and care and devotion. It wasn't a love-sick letter, but it was one of them strong, tender, *fetching* letters. It was unselfish, it asked very little of me, and offered a good deal.

"I thought over it all night, and decided at last to go. What better was I than this woman? Surely she was better educated, better bred. She had made one mistake, I had made many. She had no friends on earth; I didn't seem to have any, either. I hadn't had a letter from either of my married sisters for six or eight years, then. We could trust one another, and have an object in life in the education of the child. I'd be no worse off than I was, anyway.

"The next morning I felt better. I got ready to leave, bid all my fellow flat-wheels good-by; and had a gig ordered to take me to the train—the doctor had given me two-hundred dollars a short time before—'from a lady friend.'

"As I sat waiting for the hack, they brought me a letter from home—a big one, with a picture in it. It was from my youngest sister, and the picture was of her ten-year boy, named for me—such a happy, sunny little Swede face you never see. 'He always talks of Uncle Oscar as a great and good man,' wrote Carrie, 'and says every day that he's going to do just like you. He will do nothing that we tell him Uncle Oscar would not like, and anything that he would. If you are as good as he thinks you are, you are sure of heaven.'

"And I was even then going off to live with a woman who made a fortune out of Virginia City dance-houses. I had a sort of a remorseful chill, and before I really knew just where I was, I had got to Arizona, and from there to the Santa Fé where you knew me.

"I wrote my benefactress an honest letter, and told her why I had not come, and in a short time sent her the money she had put up for me; but it was returned again, and I sent it to the mission for my little girl.

"Well, while I was with you there, I got a fare-thee-well letter, saying that when I got that Mabel Verne would be no more—same as dead—and that she had deposited forty thousand dollars in the Phoenix Bank for *your* little girl—*yours,* mind ye—and asked me to adopt her legally and tell her that her mother was dead.

"John, I ain't heard of that woman from then until now. I thought she had got tired of waiting on me and got married, but I believe she is dead.

"I went to California and adopted the baby—a daisy too—and I've honestly tried to be a father to her.

"I got to making money in outside speculations, and had plenty; so I let her money accumulate at the Phoenix and paid her way myself.

"About four years ago, I left the road for good; bought me a nice place just outside of Oakland, and settled down to take a little comfort.

"Mabel, my daughter Mabel, for she called me papa, went to Germany, nearly three years ago, in charge of her music teacher, Sister Florence, to finish herself off. Ah, John, you ort to see her claw ivory! Before she went, she called me into the mission parlor, one day, and almost got me into a snap; she wanted me to tell her all about her parents right then, and asked me if there wasn't some mystery about her birth, and the way she happened to be left in the mission all her life, her mother disappearing, and my adoption of her."

"What did you tell her, Gun?" I asked.

"Why, lied to her, of course, as any honorable man would have done. I told her that her father was an engineer and a friend of mine, and that he was killed in an accident before she was born—that was all plausible enough.

"Then I told her that her mother was in poor health, and had died just before I had adopted her, and had left a will, giving her to me, and besides had left forty thousand dollars in the bank for her, when she married or became of age.

"Well, John, cutting down short, she met a fellow over there, a New Yorker, that just seemed to think she was made a-purpose for him, and about a year ago he wrote and asked me for my daughter—just think of it! His petition was seconded by the baby herself, and recommended by Sister Florence.

"They came home six months ago, and the baby got ready for dress-parade; and I went down to New York and seen 'em off; but here's where old Fate gets in his work again. That rascal of an O. B. Sanderson—I didn't notice the name before—was my own nephew, the very young cuss whose picture kept me from marryin' the baby's mother! I never tumbled till I ran across his mother, she was my sister Carrie.

"John, I don't care a continental cuss how good he was, the baby was good enough for him—too good—I just said nothing—and watched the signals. You ort to a seen me a-givin' the bride away! Then, when it was all over, and I was childless, I give my little girl a check for forty-seven thousand and a fraction; kissed her, and lit out for home—and here I am.

"But I ain't satisfied now, and just as quick as I get back, I'm a-going running again; then, when I've got so old I can't see more'n a car length, I'm going to ask for a steam-pump to run. I'm a-going to die railroading."

"Have you ever made any inquiries about the mother, Gun?" I asked.

"No; not much; it's so long now, it ain't no use; I guess that her light's gone out."

"What would you do, if she was to turn up?"

"Well, I don't know; I guess I'd keep still and see what she done."

"Suppose, Gun, that she showed up now; loved you more than ever for what you have done, and renewed her old proposal? You know it's leap year."

"Well, old man, if an angel flew down out of the sky and give me a second-hand pair of wings just rebuilt, and ordered me to put 'em on and follow her, I guess I wouldn't refuse to go out. Time was, though, when I'd a-held out for new, gold-mounted ones, or nothing; but that won't come, John; but you just ort to a been to the consolidation; it was just simply—well, pulling the president's special would be just like hauling a gravel-train to it!"

The train stopped suddenly here, and "Gun" said he was going ahead to get acquainted with the water-boiler, and I took out my note-book and jotted down a few points.

After the train got into motion again, I was reading over my notes, when, without looking, I thought Gunderson had come back, and I moved along in the seat to give him room, but a black dress sat down beside me.

We had been sitting with our backs to a curtain between the first berth and a stateroom. The lady came from the state-room.

"Pardon me, sir," she said, "I want to finish that story. I have heard it all; I am Sister Florence, music teacher to Mr. Gunderson's daughter; he does not know that I am on this train.

"Mr. Gunderson did not tell you that the Phoenix bank failed some months ago, and that the fortune of his adopted child was lost. He never told her and she does not know it to-day—"

"He said he paid her the full amount—" I interrupted.

"Very true. He did; but he paid it out of

his own pocket. Sold his farm; put up all his securities, and borrowed seven hundred dollars to make the sum complete. That is the reason he is going to run an engine again. He does not know that I am aware of this, so don't mention it to him."

"Gun is a man," said I; "a great, big-hearted, true man."

"He is a nobleman!" said the nun, arising and going back into the state-room.

Half an hour later, Gunderson came back, took a seat beside me and commenced to talk.

"Say, John, that's the hardest-riding old pelter I ever see, about three inches of slack between engine and tank, pounding like a stamp-mill and—" looking over his shoulder and then at me, "John, I could a swore there was some one standing right there, I *felt* 'em.

"It seems to me they ort to keep up their engines here in pretty good shape. They've got bad water, and so much boiler work that they have to have new flues before the machinery gets worn much. But, Lord, they don't seem—" he looked over his shoulder again, quickly, then settled in his seat to resume, when a pair of hands covered Gun's eyes—the nun's hands.

"Guess who it is, Gun," said I; and noticed that he was very pale.

"It's Mabel," said he, putting up his hands and taking both of hers; "no one but her ever made me feel like that."

Mormon Joe, the Robber

MORMON JOE, THE ROBBER

I'M on intimate terms with one of the biggest robbers in this country. He's an expert at the business, but has now retired from active work. The fact of the matter is, Joe didn't know he was robbing, at the time he did it, but he got there, just the same, and come mighty nigh doing time in the penitentiary for it, too.

Maybe I'd better commence at the beginning and tell you that I first knew Joe Hogg in '79, out at the front, on the Santa Fé. Joe hailed from Salt Lake City, and had run on the Utah Central, which gave him the nickname of "Mormon Joe," a name he never resented being called, and to which he always answered. I never did really know whether he was a Mormon or not, and never cared; he was a good engineer, that's about all I cared for. Joe took good care of his engine, wore a clean shirt and behaved himself—which was doing more than the average engineer at the front did.

I remember, one night, Jack McCabe—"Whisky Jack," we used to call him—made some mean remark about the Mormons in general and Joe in particular, and Joe replied: "I don't propose to defend the Mormon faith; it's as good as any, to my mind. I don't propose to judge or misjudge any man by his belief or absence of belief. All that I have got to say is, that the Mormon religion is a *practical* religion. They don't give starving women a tract, or tramps jobs on the stone-pile. The women get bread, and the tramps work for *pay*. Their faith is based on the Christian Bible, with a book added—guess they have as big a right to add or take away as some of the old kings had—bigamy is upheld by the Bible, but has been dead in Utah, for some years. It can't live for the young people are against it. In Utah the woman has all the rights a man has, votes, and is a *person*. (Since cut out of new constitution.) Before the Gentiles came to Salt Lake, the Mormons had but *one* policeman, no jail, few saloons, no houses of prostitution—now the Gentile Christian has sway, and the town is full of them. I guess you could argue on the quality and quantity of rot-gut whisky a good engineer ought to drink, better than on theology, anyhow."

I never heard any of the gang twit Joe about the Mormons again.

I didn't take an awful sight of notice about Joe until I came in, one night, and the boys told me that Joe was arrested as an accomplice in the robbery of the Black Prince mine, in Constitution gulch.

This Black Prince was a gold placer owned by two middle-aged Englishmen. They had a small stamp-mill, run by mule power; and a large number of sluice-boxes. They always worked alone, and said they were developing the mine. No one had any idea that they were taking out much dust, until the mill and sluice-boxes were burned one night, and the story came out that they had been robbed of more than thirty thousand dollars.

Each partner accused the other of the theft. Both were arrested, and detectives commenced to follow every clue.

Joe's arrest fell like a thunder-clap among us. The Brotherhood men took it up right away, and I went to see Joe, that very night. It was said that Joe had visited the Black Prince, the day before, and had been seen carrying away a large package, the night before the robbery.,

Joe absolutely refused to say a word for or against himself.

"The detectives got this scheme up and know what they are doing," said he; "I don't. When they get all through, you'll know how it'll come out."

To all questions as to his guilt or innocence, to every query about the crime or his arrest, he replied alike, to friend or foe:

"Ask the sheriff; he's doing this."

He was in jail a long time, but nothing was proven against him and he was finally released.

Neither of the Englishmen could fasten the crime on his partner, and they sold out and drifted away, one going back to England and the other to Mexico.

Joe ran awhile on the road again and then took a job as chief-engineer of a big stamp-mill in Arizona, and going there he was lost to myself and the men on the road, and finally the Black Prince robbery passed into history, and nothing remained but the tradition, a sort of a myth of the mountains, like Captain Kidd's treasures, the amount only being increased by time. I believe that the last time I heard the story, it was calmly stated that thirty million dollars was taken.

When I was out West, last time, I got off the train at Santa Fé, and when gunning through the baggage for my *kiester,* I saw a trunk, bearing on its end this legend:

"MRS. JOS. HOGG."

While I was "gopping" at it, as they say down East, and wondering if it could be my Joe Hogg, a very nice-looking lady came in, leading a little girl, glanced along the lines of trunks, put her hand on the one I was looking at, and said:

"That's the one; yes; the little one. I want it checked to New York."

Just then, a little fellow with whiskers on his chin and a twinkle in his eye came in and took charge of the trunk, the woman and the child, and with the little one's arms around his neck, bid them good-by, and got them into their seats in the sleeper.

I watched this individual with a great deal of interest; he looked like my old friend, "Mormon Joe," only for the whiskers and the stockman clothes.

Finally he jumped off the moving train, waved his hand and stood watching it out of sight, to catch the last glimpse of (to him) precious burden-bearer; he raised his hand to shade his eyes, and as he did so, I saw that it was minus one thumb, and I remembered that "Mormon Joe" left one of his under an engine up in Colorado—I was sure of him.

There was a tear in his eye, as he turned to go away, so I stepped up to him and asked:

"Any new wives wanted down your way, Elder?"

He glanced up, half angry, looked me straight in the eye, and a smile started at the southeast corner of his phiz and ran around to his port ear.

"Well, John, old man, I don't mind being *sealed* to one about your size, right now. I've just sent away the best one in the wide world. Old man, you're looking plump; by the Holy Joe Smith, a sight of you is good for sore eyes!"

Well, we started, and—but there ain't no use in telling you all about it—I went home with Joe, went up a creek with a jaw-breaking Spanish name, for miles, to a very good cattle ranch, that was the property of "Mormon Joe."

Joe only quit running some three or four years ago, and the ranch and its neat little home represented the savings of Joe Hogg's life.

His wife and only child had just started for a visit to England where she was born.

The next day we rode the range to see

Joe's cattle, and the next we started out for a little hunt. It was sitting by a jolly campfire, back in the hills of New Mexico, that "Mormon Joe" told me the true story of the robbery of the Black Prince mine and the romance of his life.

Filling his cob pipe with cut-plug, Joe sat looking away over space toward our hobbled horses and then said:

"Old man, I reckon you remember all about the Black Prince robbery. I don't forget you were the first man that came to the cooler to see me while I was doing time as a *suspect*. Well, coming right down to the point, *I had the dust all the time!* and the working out of the mystery would be rather interesting reading if it was written up, and, as you are such an accomplished liar, I wouldn't be surprised if you made it the base-line of one of them yarns of yourn— only, mind you, don't go too far with it, for it's as curious as a lie itself. I would not try to improve on it, if I was you. I'll tell it to you as it was.

"About four days before the robbery, I

was introduced to Rachel Rokesby, daughter of one of the partners in the Black Prince. I met her, in what seemed to be a casual way, at Mother Cameron's hash-foundry, but I found out, a long time afterward, that she had worked for two weeks to bring about the introduction.

"I don't know as you remember seeing her, but she was a quiet, retiring, well-educated, rosy-cheeked English girl—impressed you right away as being the pure, unrefined article, about twenty-two karat. She "chinned" me about an hour, that evening, and just cut a cameo of her pretty face right on my old heart.

"Well, course I saw her home, and tried my best to be interesting, but if a fellow ever in his natural life becomes a double-barreled jackass, it's just immediately after he falls in love. Why, he ain't as interesting as the unlettered side of an ore-sack.

"But we got on amazing well; the girl did most of the talking and along toward the last, mentioned that she was in great trouble—of course I wa'n't interested in that at all. I liked to have broken my neck in getting her to tell me at once if I couldn't do something to help her, say, for instance, move Raton mountain up agin Pike's Peak.

"I went home that night, promising to call on her the next trip, not to let any one know I was coming, not to tell anybody I had been there, not for *worlds* to repeat or intimate what she told me, and she would tell me her trouble from start to finish, and then I could help her, if I wanted to. Well, I wanted to, *bad*.

"I went up to the Rokesby's cabin, next trip in; it was dark, and as I went up the front walk, I heard the old gentleman going out the back, bound for the village 'diggin's.' I had it all to myself—the secret, I mean.

"When I went in, I got about a forty-second squeeze of a neat little hand, and things did look so nice and clean and homelike that I had it on the end of my tongue to ask right then to camp in the place.

"After a few commonplaces, she turned around and asked me if I still wanted to help her and would keep the secret, if I concluded in the end to keep out of her troubles. You bet your life, old man, she didn't have to wait long for assurance—why I wouldn't'a waited a minute to have contracted to turn the Mississippi into the Mammoth Cave, if she had asked it.

" 'Well,' says she, finally, "it is not generally known, in fact, isn't known at all, that the Black Prince is a paying placer, and that papa and Mr. Sanson have been taking out lots of gold for some time. They have over fifty pounds of gold-dust and nuggets hidden under the floor of the old mill.'

" 'Well,' says I, 'that hadn't ought to worry you so.'

" 'But that isn't all the story,' she continued; 'we have discovered a plot on the part of Mr. Sanson to rob papa of the gold and burn the mill and sluice-boxes, to hide the crime. You will find that every tough in town is his friend, because he buys whisky for them, and they all dislike papa. If he carried out his plan, we would have no redress whatever; all the justices in town can be bribed. The plan is to take the gold, burn the mill, and then accuse papa of the crime. Now, can't you help me to fool that old villain of a Sanson, and put papa's half of the money in a safe place?'

"I thought quite a while before I answered; it seemed strange to me that the case should be as she stated, and I half feared I might be made a cat's-paw and get into trouble, but the girl looked at me so trustingly with her blue eyes and added:

" 'I am afraid that I am the cause of all the trouble, too. Papa and Sanson got along well until I refused to marry him; after that, the row began—I hate him. He said I would *have* to marry him before he was done with me—but I won't!'

" 'You bet you won't, darling,' says I, before I thought. 'Pardon me, Miss Rokesby, but if there is any marrying done around here, I want a hand in the game myself.'

"She blushed deeply, looked at the toe of her shoe a minute, and said:

" 'I'm only eighteen, and am too young to think of marrying. Suppose we don't talk of that until we get out of the present difficulties.'

" 'Sensible idea,' says I. 'But when we are out, suppose you and I have a talk on that subject.'

"She looked at the toe of her shoe for a minute again, turned red and white around the gills, looked up at me, shyly at first, then fully and fairly, stretched out her hand and said:

" 'Yes; if you care to.'

"Course, I didn't *care,* or nothing—no more than a man cares for his head.

"I guess that was about a half engagement, anyhow, it's the only one we ever had. She said it would be ruinous to our plans if I was seen with her then or afterward; and agreed to leave a note at the house for me by next trip, telling me her plan—which she should talk over with her father.

"A couple of days later I got in from a round trip and made a dive for the boarding-house.

" 'Any mail for me, mother?' I asked old Mrs. Cameron.

Read — John 3:16

"'No, young man; I'm sorry to say there ain't'

"'I was anxious to hear from home.'

"'Too bad; but maybe it'll come to-morrow.'

"I was up to fever heat, but could do nothing but wait. I went to bed late, and, raising up my pillow to put my watch under it, I found a note; it read:

"'Midnight, July 17.
"'DEAR JOE:

"'Just thought of that rule for changing counter-balance you wanted. There has always been a miscalculation about the weight of counter-balance; they are universally *too heavy*. The weights are in pieces; take out two *pieces;* this treatment would even improve a mule sweep. When once out, pieces should be changed or placed where careless or malicious persons cannot get hold of them and replace them. All is well; hope you are the same; will see you some time soon.

"'JACK.'

"Here was apparently a fool letter from one young railroader to another, but I knew well enough that it was from Rachel and meant something.

"I noticed that it was dated the *next night;* then I commenced to see, and in a few minutes my instructions were plain. The old five-stamp mill was driven by a mule, who wandered aimlessly around a never-ending circle at the end of a long, wooden sweep; this pole extended past the post of the mill a few feet, and had on the short end a box of stones as a counter-weight. I would find two packages of gold there at midnight of July 17.

"I was running one of those old Pittsburgh hogs then, and she had to have her throttle ground the next day, but it was more than likely that she would be ready to go out at 8:30 on her turn; but I arranged to have it happen that the stand-pipe yoke should be broken in putting it up, so that another engine would have to be fired up, and I would lay in.

"I told stories in the roundhouse until nearly ten o'clock that fateful night, and then started for the hash-foundry, dodged into a lumber yard, got onto the rough ground back of town and made a wide detour toward Constitution Gulch, the Black Prince and the mule-sweep. I crept up to the washed ground through some brush and laid down in a path to wait for midnight. I felt a full-fledged sneak-thief, but I thought of Rachel and didn't care if I was one or not, so long as she was satisfied.

"I looked often at my watch in the moonlight, and at twelve o'clock everything was as still as death. I could hear my own heart beat against my ribs as I sneaked up to that counter-balanced sweep. I got there without accident or incident, found two packages done up in canvas with tarred-string handles; they were heavy but small, and in ten minutes I had them alone with me among the stumps and stones on the little *mesa* back of town.

"I'll never forget how I felt there in the dark with all that money that wasn't mine, and if some one had have said 'boo' from behind a stump, I should have probably dropped the boodle and taken to the brush.

"As I approached the town, I realized that I could never get through it to the boarding-house or the roundhouse with those two bundles that *looked like country sausages.* I studied awhile on it and finally put them under an old scraper beside the road, and went without them to the shops. I got from my seat-box a clean pair of overalls and jacket and came back without being seen.

"I wrapped one of the packages up in these and boldly stepped out into the glare of the electric lights—I remember I thought the town too darned enterprising.

"One of the first men I met was the marshal, Jack Kelly. He was reported to be a Pinkerton man, and was mistrusted by some of the men, but tried to be friendly and 'stand in' with all of us. He slapped me on the back and nearly scared the wits out of me. He insisted on treating me, and I went into a saloon and 'took something' with him, in fear and trembling. The package was heavy, but I must carry it lightly under my arm, as if it were only overclothes.

"I treated in return, and had it charged,

because I dare not attempt to get my right hand into my pocket. Jack was disposed to talk, and I feared he was just playing with me like a cat does with a mouse, but I finally got off and deposited my precious burden in my seat-box, under lock and key—then I sneaked back for the second haul. I met Jack and a policeman, on my next trip, and he exclaimed:

"'Why, ain't you gone out yet?' and started off, telling the roundsman to keep the bunkos off me up to the shop. *I thought then I was caught,* but I was not, and the bluecoat bid me a pleasant good-night, at the shop yard.

"When I got near my engine, I was surprised to see Barney Murry, the night machinist, with his torch up on the cab—he was putting in the newly-ground throttle.

"Just before I had decided to emerge from the shadow of the next engine, Barney commenced to yell for his helper, Dick, to come and help him on with the dome-cover.

"Dick came with a sandwich in one hand and a can of coffee in the other. This reminded Barney of his lunch, and setting his torch down on the top of the cab, he scrambled down on the other side and hurried off to the sand-dryer, where the gang used to eat their dyspepsia insurance and swap lies.

"After listening a moment, to be sure I was alone, I stepped lightly to the cab, and in a minute the two heavy and dangerous packages were side by side again.

"But just here an inspiration struck me. I opened the front door of the cab, stepped out on the running-board, and a second later was holding Barney's smoking torch down in the dome.

"The throttle occupied most of the space, but there was considerable room each side of it and a good two feet between the top of the boiler shell and the top row of flues. I took one of the bags of gold, held it down at arm's length, swung it backward and forward a time or two, and let go, so as to drop it well ahead on the flues: the second bag followed at once, and again I held down the light to see if the bags were out of sight; satisfied on this point, I got down, took my clothes under my arm, and jumped off the engine into the arms of the night foreman."

" 'What did you call me for? That engine is not ready to go out on the extra,' I demanded, off-hand.

" 'I ain't called you; you're dreaming.'

" 'May be I am,' said I, 'but I would 'a swore some one came and called under my window that I got out at 2:10, on a stock-train, extra.'

"Just then, Barney and Dick came back, and I soon had the satisfaction of seeing the cover screwed down on my secret and a fire built under it—then I went home and slept.

"I guess it was four round trips that I made with the old pelter, before Kelly put this and that together, and decided to put me where the dogs wouldn't bite me.

"I appeared as calm as I could, and set the example since followed by politicians, that of 'dignified silence.' Kelly tried to work one of the 'fellow convict' rackets on me, but I made no confessions. I soon became a martyr, in the eyes of the women of the town. You boys got to talking of backing up a suit for false imprisonment; election was coming on and the sheriff and county judge were getting uneasy, and the district attorney was awfully unhappy, so they let me out.

"Nixon, the sheriff, pumped me slyly, to see what effect my imprisonment would have on future operations, and I told him I didn't propose to lose any time over it, and agreed to drop the matter for a little nest-egg equal to the highest pay received by any engineer on the road. Pat Dailey was the worst hog for overtime, and I selected his pay as the standard and took big money,—from the campaign funds. I wasn't afraid of re-arrest;—I had 'em for bribery.

"Whilst I was in hock, I had cold chills every time I heard the 313's whistle, for fear they would wash her out and find the dust; but she gave up nothing.

"When I reported for work, the old scrap was out on construction and they were disposed to put me on another mill, pulling varnished cars, but I told the old man I was under the weather and 'crummy,' and that put him in a good humor; and I was sent out to a desolate siding, and once again took charge of the steam 'fence,' for the robber of the Black Prince mine.

"On Sunday, by a little maneuvering, I managed to get the crew to go off on a trout-fishing expedition, and under pretext of grinding-in her chronically leaky throttle, I took off her dome-cover and looked in; there was nothing in sight.

"I was afraid that the cooking of two months or more had destroyed the canvas bags; then again the heavy deposit of scale might have cemented the bags to the flues. In either case, rough handling would send the dust to the bottom of the boiler, making it difficult if not impossible to recover; and worse yet, manifest itself sometime and give me dead away.

"I concluded to go at the matter right, and after two hours of hard work, managed to get the upright throttle-pipe out of the dome. I drew her water down below the flue-line, and though it was tolerably warm, I got in.

"Both of my surmises were partially correct; the canvas was rotted, in a measure, and the bags were fastened to the flues. The dust had been put up in buckskin bags, first, and these had been put into shot-sacks; the buckskin was shrunken but intact. I took a good look around, before I dared take the treasure into the sunlight; but the coast was clear, and inside of an hour they were locked in my clothes-box, and the cover was on the kettle again and I was pumping her up by hand.

"I was afraid something would happen to me or the engine, so I buried the packages in a bunch of willows near the track.

"It must have been two weeks after this that a mover's wagon stopped near the creek within half a mile of the track, and hobbled horses soon began to 'rustle' grass, and the smoke of a camp-fire hunted the clouds.

"We saw this sort of thing often, and I didn't any more than glance at it; but after supper I sauntered down by the engine, smoking and thinking of Rachel Rokesby, when I noticed a woman walking towards me, pail in hand.

"She had on a sunbonnet that hid her face

and she got within ten feet of me before she spoke—she asked for a pail of drinking-water from the tank—the creek was muddy from a recent rain.

"Just as soon as she spoke, I knew it was Rachel, but I controlled myself, for others were within hearing. I walked with her to the engine and got the water; I purposely drew the pail full, which she promptly spilled, and I offered to carry it for her.

"The crew watched us walk away and I heard some of them mention 'mash,' but I didn't care, I wanted a word with my girl.

"When we were out of earshot, she asked without looking up:

"'Well, old coolness, are you all right?'

"'You bet! darling.'

"'Papa has sold out his half and we are going away for good. I think if we get rid of the dust without trouble, we may go to England. Just as soon as all is safe, you shall hear from me; can't you trust me, Joe?'

"'Yes, Rachel, darling; now and forever.'

"'Where's the gold?'

"'Within one hundred feet of you, in

those willows; when it is dark, I will go and get it and put it on that stump by the big tree; go then and get it. But where will you put it?'

" 'I'm going to pack it in the bottom of a jar of butter.'

" 'Good idea, little girl! I think you'd make a good thief yourself. How's my friend, Sanson?'

" 'He's gone to Mexico; says yet that papa robbed him, but he knows as well as you or I that all his bluster was because he only found *half* that he expected; I pride myself on getting ahead of a wicked man once, thanks to our hero, by the name of Hogg.'

"It was getting dusk and we were out of sight, so I sat down the pail and asked:

" 'Do I get a kiss, this evening?'

" 'If you want one.'

" 'There's only one thing I want worse.'

" 'What is that, Joe?'

"My arm was around her waist now, and the sunbonnet was shoved back from the face. I took a couple of cream-puffs where they were ripe, and answered:

"'That message to come and have that talk about matrimony.'

"Here a man's voice was heard calling: 'Rachel! Rachel!' and throwing her arms around my neck, she gave me one more kiss, snatched up her pail and answered:

"'Yes; I'm coming.'

"Then to me, hurriedly:

"'Good-by, dear; wait patiently, you shall hear from me.'

"I went back and put the dangerous dust on the stump and returned to the bunk-car. The next morning when I turned out, the outlines of the wagon were dimly discernible away on a hill in the road; it had been gone an hour.

"I walked down past my stump—the gold was gone.

"Well, John, I settled down to work and to wait for that precious letter that would summon me to the side of Rachel Rokesby, wherever she was; but it never came. Uncle Sam never delivered a line to me from her from that day to this."

Joe kicked the burning sticks in our fire

closer together, lit his pipe and then proceeded:

"I was hopeful for a month or two; then got impatient, and finally got angry, but it ended in despair. A year passed away before I commenced to *hunt,* instead of waiting to be hunted; but after another year I gave it up, and came to the belief that Rachel was dead or married to another. But the very minute that such a treasonable thought flashed through my mind, my heart held up the image of her pure face and rebuked me.

"I was discharged finally, for forgetting orders—I was thinking of something else— then I commenced to pull myself together and determined to control myself. I held the job in Arizona almost a year, but the mill company busted; then I drifted down on to the Mexican National, when it was building, and got a job. A few months later, it came to my ears that one of our engineers, Billy Gardiner, was in one of their damnable prisons, for running over a Greaser, and I organized a relief expedition. I called on Gardiner, and talked over his trouble fully;

he was in a loathsome dobie hole, full of vermin, and dark. As I sat talking to him, I noticed an old man, chained to the wall in a little entry on the other side of the room. His beard was grizzly white, long and tangled. He was hollow-cheeked and wild-eyed, and looked at me in a strange, fascinated way.

" 'What's he in for,' I whispered to Gardiner.

" 'Murdered his partner in a mining camp. Got caught in the act. He don't know it yet, but he's condemned to be shot next Friday—to-morrow. Poor devil, he's half crazy, anyhow.'

"As I got up to go, the old man made a sharp hiss, and as I turned to look at him, he beckoned with his finger. I took a step or two nearer, and he asked, in an audible whisper:

" 'Mr. Hogg, don't you know me?'

"I looked at him long and critically, and then said:

" 'No; I never saw you before.'

" 'Yes; that's so,' said he; 'but I have

seen you, many times. You remember the Black Prince robbery?'

" 'Yes, indeed; then you are Sanson?'

" 'No; Rokesby.'

" 'Rokesby! My God, man, where's Rachel?'

" 'I thought so,' he muttered. 'Well, she's in England, but I'm here.'

" 'What part of England?'

" 'Sit down on that box, Mr. Hogg, and I will tell you something.'

" 'Is she married?' I asked eagerly.

" 'No, lad, she ain't, and what's more, she won't be till she marries you, so be easy there.'

"Just here a pompous Mexican official strode in, stepped up in front of the old man and read something in Spanish.

" 'What in hell did he say?' asked the prisoner of Gardiner.

" 'Something about sentence, pardner.'

" 'Well, it's time they was doing something; did he say when it was?'

" 'To-morrow.'

" 'Good enough; I'm dead sick o' this.'

"'Can't I do anything for you, Mr. Rokesby— for Rachel's sake?'

"'No—yes, you can, too, young man; you can grant me a pardon for a worse crime nor murder, if you will—for—for Rachel's sake."

"'It's granted then.'

"'Good! that gives me heart. Now, Mr. Hogg, to business, it was me that robbed the Black Prince mine. I took every last cent there was, and I used you and Rachel to do the work for me and take the blame if caught. Sanson was honest enough, I fired the mill myself.

"'It was me that sent Rachel to you; I admired your face, as you rode by the claim every day on your engine. I knew you had nerve. If you and Rachel hadn't fallen in love with one another, I'd 'a lost though; but I won.

"'Well, I took the money I got for the claim and sent Rachel back to her mother's sister, in England. You may not know, but she is not my daughter; she thinks she is, though. Her parents died when she was small, and I provided for her. I'm her half-uncle. I got avaricious in my old age, and went into a number of questionable schemes.

" 'After leaving New Mexico, I worked the dust off, a little at a time, an' wasted the money—but never mind that.

" 'It was just before she got aboard the ship that Rachel sent me a letter containing another to you, to be sent when all was right —I've carried it ever since—somehow or other I was afraid it would drop a clew to send it at first, and after it got a year old, I didn't think of it much.'

"He fumbled around inside of his dirty flannel shirt for a minute, and soon fished up a letter almost as black as the shirt, and holding it up, said:

" 'That's it.'

" 'I had the envelope off in a second, and read:

" 'DEAR JOSEPH:
" 'I am going to my aunt, Mrs. Julia Bradshaw, 15 Harrow Lane, Leicester, England. If you do not change your mind, I will be

happy to talk over our affairs whenever you are ready. I shall be waiting.

"'RACHEL.'

"I turned and bolted toward a door, when Gardiner yelled:

"'Where are you going?'

"'To England,' said I.

"'This door, then, sir,' said a Mexican.

"I came back to the old man.

"'Rokesby,' said I, 'you have cut ten years off my life, but I forgive you; good-by.'

"'One thing more, Mr. Hogg; don't tell 'em at home how I went—nothing about this last deal.'

"'Well, all right; but I'll tell Rachel, if we marry and come to America.'

"'I've got lots of honest relations, and my old mother still lives, in her eighties.'

"'Well, not till after she goes, unless to save Rachel in some way.'

"'Good-by, Mr. Hogg, God bless you! and —and, little Rachel.'

"'Good-by, Mr. Rokesby.'

"The next day I left Mexico for God's

country, and inside of ten days was on a Cunarder, eastward bound. I reached England in proper time; I found the proper pen in the proper train, and was deposited in the proper town, directed to the proper house, and street, and number, and had pulled out about four yards of wire attached to the proper bell.

"A kindly-faced old lady looked at me over her spectacles, and I asked:

" 'Does Mrs. Julia Bradshaw live here?'

" 'Yes, sir; that's me.'

" 'Have you a young lady here named Rachel R—'

"The old lady didn't wait for me to finish the name, she just turned her head fifteen degrees, put her open hand up beside her mouth, and shouted upstairs:

" 'Rachel! Rachel! Come down here, quick! Here's your young man from America!' "

A Midsummer Night's Trip

A MIDSUMMER NIGHT'S TRIP

It is all of twenty years now since the little incident happened that I am going to tell you about. After the strike of '77, I went into exile in the wild and woolly West, mostly in "bleeding Kansas," but often in Colorado, New Mexico, and Arizona—the Santa Fé goes almost everywhere in the Southwest.

One night in August I was dropping an old Baldwin consolidator down a long Mexican grade, after having helped a stock train over the division by double-heading. It was close and hot on this sage-brush waste, something not unusual at night in high altitudes, and the heat and sheet lightning around the horizon warned me that there was to be one of those short, fierce storms that come but once or twice a year in these latitudes, and which are known as cloudbursts.

The alkali plains, or deserts, as they are

often erroneously called, are great stretches of adobe soil, known as "dobie" by the natives. This soil is a yellowish brown, or perhaps more of a gray color, and as fine as flour. Water plays sad havoc with it, if the soil lies so as to oppose the flow, and it moves like dust before a slight stream. On the flat, hard-baked plains, the water makes no impression, but on a railroad grade, be it ever so slight, the tendency is to dig pitfalls. I have seen a little stream of water, just enough to fill the ditches on each side of the track, take out all the dirt, and keep the ties and track afloat until the water was gone, then drop them into a hole eight or ten feet deep, or if the wash-out was short, leave them suspended, looking safe and sound, to lure some poor engineer and his mate to death.

Another peculiarity of these storms is that they come quickly, rage furiously for a few minutes, and are gone, and their lines are sharply defined. It is not uncommon to find a lot of water, or a wash-out, within a mile of land so dry that it looks as if it had never seen a drop of water.

All this land is fertile when it can be brought under irrigating ditches and watered, but here it lies out almost like a desert. It is sparsely inhabited along the little streams by a straggling off-shoot of the Mexican race; yet once in a while a fine place is to be seen, like an oasis in the Sahara, the home of some old Spanish Don, with thousands of cattle or sheep ranging on the plains, or perhaps the headquarters of some enterprising cattle company. But these places were few and far between at the time of which I write; the stations were mere passing places, long side-tracks, with perhaps a stock-yard and section house once in a while, but generally without buildings or even switch lights.

Noting the approach of the storm, I let the heavy engine drop the faster, hoping to reach a certain side-track, over twenty miles away, where there was a telegraph operator, and learn from him the condition of the road. But the storm was faster than any consolidator that Baldwins ever built, and as the lightning suddenly ceased and the air became heavy, hot, and absolutely motionless, I realized that we would have the storm full upon us in a few moments. I had nothing to meet for more than thirty miles, and there was nothing behind me; so I stopped, turned the headlight up, and hung my white signal lamps down below the buffer-beams each side of the pilot—this to enable me to see the ends of the ties and the ditch.

Billy Howell, my fireman, and a good one, hastily went over the boiler-jacket with signal oil, to prevent rust; we donned our gum coats; I dropped a little oil on the "Mary Ann's" gudgeon's, and we proceeded on our way without a word. On these big consolidators you cannot see well ahead, past the big boiler, from the cab, and I always ran with my head out of the side window. Both of us took this position now, standing up ready for anything; but we bowled safely along for one mile—two miles, through the awful hush. Then, as sudden as a flash of light, "boom!" went a peal of thunder as sharp and clear as a signal gun. There was a flash of light along the rails, the surface of the desert seemed to break out here and there with little fitful jets of greenish-blue flame, and from every side came the answering reports from the batteries of heaven, like sister gun-boats answering a salute. The rain fell in torrents, yes, in sheets. I have never, before or since, seen such a grand and fantastic display of fireworks, nor heard such rivalry of cannonade. I stopped my engine, and looked with awe and interest at this angry fit of nature, watched the balls of fire play along the ground, and realized for the first time what a sight was an electric storm.

As the storm commenced at the signal of a mighty peal of thunder, so it ended as suddenly at the same signal; the rain changed in an instant from a torrent to a gentle shower, the lightning went out, the batteries ceased their firing, the breeze commenced to blow gently, the air was purified. Again we heard the signal peal of thunder, but it seemed a great way off, as if the piece was hurrying away to a more urgent quarter. The gentle shower ceased, the black clouds were torn asunder overhead; invisible hands seemed to snatch a gray veil of fleecy clouds from the face of the harvest moon, and it shone out as clear and serene as before the storm. The ditches on each side of the track were half full of water, ties were floating along in them, but the track seemed safe and sound, and we proceeded cautiously on our way. Within two miles the road turned to the West, and here we found the water in the ditches running through dry soil, carrying dead grass and twigs of sage upon its surface; we passed the head of the flood, tumbling along through the dry ditches as dirty as it well could be, and fast soaking into the soil; and then we passed beyond the line of the storm entirely.

Billy put up his seat and filled his pipe, and I sat down and absorbed a sandwich as I urged my engine ahead to make up for lost time; we took up our routine of work just where we had left it, and—life was the same old song. It was past midnight now, and as

I never did a great deal of talking on an engine, I settled down to watching the rails ahead, and wondering if the knuckle-joints would pound the rods off the pins before we got to the end of the division.

Billy, with his eyes on the track ahead, was smoking his second pipe and humming a tune, and the "Mary Ann" was making about forty miles an hour, but doing more rolling and pitching and jumping up and down than an eight-wheeler would at sixty. All at once I discerned something away down the track where the rails seemed to meet. The moon had gone behind a cloud, and the headlight gave a better view and penetrated further. Billy saw it, too, for he took his pipe out of his mouth, and with his eyes still upon it, said laconically, as was his wont: "Cow."

"Yes," said I, closing the throttle and dropping the lever ahead.

"Man," said Billy, as the shape seemed to assume a perpendicular position.

"Yes," said I, reaching for the three-way cock, and applying the tender brake, without thinking what I did.

"Woman," said Billy, as the shape was seen to wear skirts, or at least drapery.

"Mexican," said I, as I noted the mantilla over the head. We were fast nearing the object.

"No," said Billy, "too well built."

I don't know what he judged by; we could not see the face, for it was turned away from us; but the form was plainly that of a comely woman. She stood between the rails with her arms stretched out like a cross, her white gown fitting her figure closely. A black, shawl-like mantilla was over the head, partly concealing her face; her right foot was upon the left-hand rail. She stood perfectly still. We were within fifty feet of her, and our speed was reduced to half, when Billy said sharply: "Hold her, John—for God's sake!"

But I had the "Mary Ann" in the back motion before the words left his mouth, and was choking her on sand. Billy leaned upon the boiler-head and pulled the whistle-cord, but the white figure did not move. I shut my eyes as we passed the spot where she had

"'*Mexican*,' said I."
(*page* 236.)

stood. We got stopped a rod or two beyond. I took the white light in the tank and sprang to the ground. Billy lit the torch, and followed me with haste. The form still stood upon the track just where we had first seen it; but it faced us and the arms were folded. I confess to hurrying slowly until Billy caught up with the torch, which he held over his head.

"Good evening, señors," said the apparition, in very sweet English, just tinged with the Castilian accent, but she spoke as if nearly exhausted.

"Good gracious," said I, "whatever brought you away out here, and hadn't you just as lief shoot a man as scare him to death?"

She laughed very sweetly, and said: "The washout brought me just here, and I fancy it was lucky for you—both of you."

"Washout?" said I. "Where?"

"At the dry bridge beyond."

Well, to make a long story short, we took her on the engine—she was wet through—and went on to the dry bridge. This was a little wooden structure in a sag, about a mile away, and we found that the storm we had encountered farther back had done bad work at each end of the bridge. We did not cross that night, but after placing signals well behind us and ahead of the washout, we waited until morning, the three of us sitting in the cab of the "Mary Ann," chatting as if we were old acquaintances.

This young girl, whose fortunes had been so strangely cast with ours, was the daughter of Señor Juan Arboles, a rich old Spanish Don who owned a fine place and immense herds of sheep over on the Rio Pecos, some ten miles west of the road. She was being educated in some Catholic school or convent at Trinidad, and had the evening before alighted at the big corrals, a few miles below, where she was met by one of her father's Mexican rancheros, who led her saddle broncho. They had started on their fifteen-mile ride in the cool of the evening, and following the road back for a few miles were just striking off toward the distant hedge of cotton woods that lined the little stream by her home when the storm came upon them.

There was a lone pine tree hardly larger than a bush about a half-mile from the track, and riding to this, the girl, whose name was Josephine, had dismounted to seek its scant protection, while the herder tried to hold the frightened horses. As peal on peal of thunder resounded and the electric lights of nature played tag over the plain, the horses became more and more unmanageable and at last stampeded, with old Paz muttering Mexican curses and chasing after them wildly.

After the storm passed, Josephine waited in vain for Paz and the bronchos, and then debated whether she should walk toward her home or back to the corrals. In either direction the distance was long, and the adobe soil is very tenacious when wet, and the wayfarer needs great strength to carry the load it imposes on the feet. As she stood there, thinking what it was best to do, a sound came to her ears from the direction of the timber and home, which she recognized in an instant, and without waiting to debate further, she turned and ran with all her strength, not toward her home, but away from it. Across the waste of stunted sage she sped, the cool breeze upon her face, every muscle strained to its utmost. Nearer and nearer came the sound; the deep, regular bay of the timber wolf. These animals are large and fierce; they do not go in packs, like the smaller and more cowardly breeds of wolves, but in pairs, or, at most, six together. A pair of them will attack a man even when he is mounted, and lucky is he if he is well armed and cool enough to despatch one before it fastens its fangs in his horse's throat or his own thigh.

As the brave girl ran, she cast about for some means of escape or place of refuge. She decided to run to the railroad track and climb a telegraph pole—a feat which, owing to her free life on the ranch, she was perfectly capable of. Once up the pole, she could rest on the cross-tree, in perfect safety from the wolves, and she would be sure to be seen and rescued by the first train that came along after daybreak.

She approached the track over perfectly dry ground. To reach the telegraph poles, she sprang nimbly into the ditch; and as she did so, she saw a stream of water coming rapidly toward her—it was the front of the flood. The ditch on the opposite side of the track, which she must also cross to reach the line of poles, she found already full-flooded. She decided to run up the track, between the walls of water. This would put a ten-foot stream between her and her pursuers, and change her course enough, she hoped, to throw them off the scent. In this design she was partly successful, for the bay of the wolves showed that they were going to the track as she had gone, instead of cutting straight across toward her. Thus she gained considerable time. She reached the little arroyo spanned by the dry bridge; it was like a mill-pond, and the track was afloat. She ran across the bridge; she scarcely slackened speed, although the ties rocked and moved on the spike-heads holding them to the rails.

She hoped for a moment that the wolves would not venture to follow her over such a way; but their hideous voices were still in her ear and came nearer and nearer. Then there came to her, faintly, another, a strange, metallic sound. What was it? Where was it? She ran on tiptoe a few paces in order to hear it better; it was in the rails—the vibration of a train in motion. Then there came into view a light—a headlight; but it was so far away, so very far, and that awful baying so close! The "Mary Ann," however, was fleeter of foot than the wolves; the light grew big and bright and the sound of working machinery came to the girl on the breeze.

Would they stop for her? Could she make them see her? Then she thought of the bridge. It was death for them as well as for her—they *must* see her. She resolved to stay on the track until they whistled her off; but now the light seemed to come so slow. A splash at her side caused her to turn her head, and there, a dozen feet away, were her pursuers, their tongues out, their eyes shining like balls of fire. They were just entering the water to come across to her. They fascinated her by their very fierceness. Forgetting where she was for the instant, she stared dumbly at them until called to life and action by a scream from the locomotive's whistle. Then she sprang from the track just in the nick of time. She actually laughed as she saw two grayish-white wolf-tails bob here and there among the sage brush, as the wolves took flight at sight of the engine.

This was the story she told as she dried her garments before the furnace door, and I confess to holding this cool, self-reliant girl in high admiration. She never once thought of fainting; but along toward morning she did say that she was scared then at thinking of it.

Early in the morning a party of herders, with Josephine's father ahead, rode into sight. They were hunting for her. Josephine got up on the tender to attract their attention, and soon she was in her father's arms. Her frightened pony had gone home as fast as his legs would carry him, and a relief party swam their horses at the ford and rode forward at once.

The old Don was profuse in his thanks, and would not leave us until Billy and I had agreed to visit his ranch and enjoy a hunt with him, and actually set a date when we should meet him at the big corral. I wanted a rest anyway, and it was perfectly plain that Billy was beyond his depth in love with the girl at first sight; so we were not hard to persuade when she added her voice to her father's.

Early in September Billy and I dropped off No. 1 with our guns and "plunder," as baggage is called there, and a couple of the old Don's men met us with saddle and pack animals. I never spent a pleasanter two weeks in my life. The quiet, almost gloomy, old Don and I became fast friends, and the hunting was good. The Don was a Spaniard, but Josephine's mother had been a Mexican woman, and one noted for her beauty. She had been dead some years at the time of our visit. Billy devoted most of his time to the

A MIDSUMMER NIGHT'S TRIP 245

girl. They were a fine looking young couple, he being strong and broad-shouldered, with laughing blue eyes and light curly hair, she slender and perfect in outline, with a typical Southern complexion, black eyes—and such eyes they were—and hair and eyebrows like the raven's wing.

A few days before Billy and I were booked to resume our duties on the deck of the "Mary Ann," Miss Josephine took my arm and walked me down the yard and pumped me quietly about "Mr. Howell," as she called Billy. She went into details a little, and I answered all questions as best I could. All I said was in the young man's favor—it could not, in truth, be otherwise. Josephine seemed satisfied and pleased.

When we got back to headquarters, I was given the care of a cold-water Hinkley, with a row of varnished cars behind her, and Billy fell heir to the rudder of the "Mary Ann." We still roomed together. Billy put in most of his lay-over time writing long letters to somebody, and every Thursday, as regular as a clock, one came for him, with a censor's mark on it. Often after reading the letter, Billy would say: "That girl has more horse sense than the rest of the whole female race —she don't slop over worth a cent." He invariably spoke of her as "my Mexican girl," and often asked my opinion about white men intermarrying with that mongrel race. Sometimes he said that his mother would go crazy if he married a Mexican, his father would disown him, and his brother Henry—well, Billy did not like to think just what revenge Henry would take. Billy's father was manager of an Eastern road, and his brother was assistant to the first vice-president, and Billy looked up to the latter as a great man and a sage. He himself was in the West for practical experience in the machinery department, and to get rid of a slight tendency to asthma. He could have gone East any time and "been somebody" on the road under his father.

Finally, Billy missed a week in writing. At once there was a cog gone from the answering wheel to match. Billy shortened his letters; the answers were shortened.

Then he quit writing, and his Thursday letter ceased to come. He had thought the matter all over, and decided, no doubt, that he was doing what was best—both for himself and the girl; that his family's high ideas should not be outraged by a Mexican marriage. He had put a piece of flesh-colored court-plaster over his wound, not healed it.

Early in the winter the old Don wrote, urging us to come down and hunt antelope, but Billy declined to go—said that the road needed him, and that Josephine might come home from school and this would make them both uncomfortable. But Henry, his older brother, was visiting him, and he suggested that I take Henry; he would enjoy the hunt, and it would help him drown his sorrow over the loss of his aristocratic young wife, who had died a year or two before. So Henry went with me, and we hunted antelope until we tired of the slaughter. Then the old Don planned a deer-hunting trip in the mountains, but I had to go back to work, and left Henry and the old Don to take the trip without me. While they were in the mountains,

Josephine came home, and Henry Howell's stay lengthened out to a month. But I did not know until long afterward that the two had met.

Billy was pretty quiet all winter, worked hard and went out but little—he was thinking about something. One day I came home and found him writing a letter. "What now, Billy?" I asked.

"Writing to my Mexican girl," said he.

"I thought you had got over that a long time ago?"

"So did I, but I hadn't. I've been trying to please somebody else besides myself in this matter, and I'm done. I'm going to work for Bill now."

"Take an old man's advice, Billy, and don't write that girl a line—go and see her."

"Oh, I can fix it all right by letter, and then run down there and see her."

"Don't do it."

"I'll risk it."

A week later Billy and I sat on the veranda of the company's hash-foundry, figuring up our time and smoking our cob meerschaums, when one of the boys who had been to the office, placed two letters in Billy's hands. One of them was directed in the handwriting that used to be on the old Thursday letters. Billy tore it open eagerly —and his own letter to Josephine dropped into his hand. Billy looked at the ground steadily for five minutes, and I pretended not to have seen. Finally he said, half to himself: "You were right, I ought to have gone myself—but I'll go now, go to-morrow." Then he opened the other letter.

He read its single page with manifest interest, and when his eyes reached the last line they went straight on, and looked at the ground, and continued to do so for fully five minutes. Without looking up, he said: "John, I want you to do me two favors."

"All right," said I.

Still keeping his eyes on the ground, he said, slowly, as if measuring everything well: "I'm going up and draw my time, and will leave for Old Mexico on No. 4 to-night. I want you to write to both these parties and tell them that I have gone there and that you have forwarded both these letters. Don't tell 'em that I went after reading 'em."

"And the other favor, Billy?"

"Read this letter, and see me off to-night."

The letter read:

"Philadelphia, May 1, 1879.

"DEAR BROTHER WILL: I want you and Mr. A. to go down to Don Juan Arboles's by the first of June. I will be there then. You must be my best man, as I stand up to marry the sweetest, dearest wild-flower of a woman that ever bloomed in a land of beauty. Don't fail me. Josephine will like you for my sake, and you will love her for your brother. HENRY."

Most engineers' lives are busy ones and full of accident and incident, and having my full share of both, I had almost forgotten all these points about Billy Howell and his Mexican girl, when they were all recalled by a letter from Billy himself. With his letter was a photograph of a family group—a be-whiskered man of thirty-five, a good-looking woman of twenty, but undoubtedly a Mexican, and a curly-headed baby, perhaps a year old The letter ran:

"City of Mexico, July 21, 1890.
"DEAR OLD JOHN: I had lost you, and thought that perhaps you had gone over to the majority, until I saw your name and recognized your quill in a story. Write to me; am doing well. I send you a photograph of all there are of the Howell outfit. *No halfbreeds for your uncle this time.*
"WM. HOWELL."

The Polar Zone

THE POLAR ZONE

VERY few of my friends know me for a seafaring man, but I sailed the salt seas, man and boy, for nine months and eighteen days, and I know just as much about sailing the hereinbefore mentioned salt seas as I ever want to.

Ever so long ago, when I was young and tender, I used to have fits of wanting to go into business for myself. Along about the front edge of the seventies, pay for "toting" people and truck over the eastern railroads of New England was not of sufficient plenitude to worry a man as to how he would invest his pay check—it was usually invested before he got it. One of my periodical fits of wanting to go into business for myself came on suddenly one day, when I got home and found another baby in the house. I was right in the very worst spasms of it when my brother Enoch, whom I hadn't seen for seventeen years, walked in on me.

Enoch was fool enough to run away to sea when he was twelve years old—I suppose he was afraid he would get the chance to do something besides whaling. We were born down New Bedford way, where another boy and myself were the only two fellows in the district, for over forty years, who didn't go hunting whales, icebergs, foul smells, and scurvy, up in King Frost's bailiwick, just south of the Pole.

Enoch had been captain and part owner of a Pacific whaler; she had recently burned at Honolulu, and he was back home now to buy a new ship. He had heard that I, his little brother John, was the best locomotive engineer in the whole world, and had come to see me—partly on account of relationship, but more to get my advice about buying a steam whaling-ship. Enoch knew more about whales and ships and such things than you could put down in a book, but he had no more idea *how* steam propelled a ship than I had what a "skivvie tricer" was.

Well, before the week was out, Enoch showed me that he was pretty well fixed in a financial way, and as he had no kin but me that he cared about, he offered me an interest in his new steam whaler, if I would go as chief engineer with her to the North Pacific.

The terms were liberal and the chance a good one, so it seemed, and after a good many consultations, my wife agreed to let me go for *one* cruise. She asked about the stops to be made in going around the Horn, and figured mentally a little after each place was named—I believe now, she half expected that I would desert the ship and walk home from one of these spots, and was figuring on the time it would take me.

When the robins were building their nests, the new steam whaler, "Champion," left New Bedford for parts unknown (*via* the Horn), with the sea-sickest chief engineer that ever smelt fish oil. The steam plant wasn't very much—two boilers and a plain twenty-eight by thirty-six double engine, and any amount of hoisting rigs, blubber boilers, and other paraphernalia. We refitted in San Francisco, and on a clear summer morning turned the white-painted figure-head of the "Champion" toward the north and stood out for Behring sea. But, while we lay at the mouth of the Yukon river, up in Alaska, getting ready for a sally into the realm of water above the Straits, a whaler, bound for San Francisco and home, dropped anchor near us, the homesickness struck in on me, and—never mind the details now—your Uncle John came home without any whales, and was mighty glad to get on the extra list of the old road.

The story I want to tell, however, is another man's story, and it was while lying in the Yukon that I heard it. I was deeply impressed with it at the time, and meant to give it to the world as soon as I got home, for I set it all down plain then, but I lost my diary, and half forgot the story—who wouldn't forget a story when he had to make two hundred and ten miles a day on a locomotive and had five children at home? But now, after twenty years, my wife turns up that old diary in the garret this spring while house-cleaning. Fred had it and an old Fourth-of-July cannon put away in an ancient valise, as a boy will treasure up useless things.

Under the head of October 12th, I find this entry:

"At anchor in Yukon river, weather fair, recent heavy rains; set out packing and filed main-rod brasses of both engines. Settled with Enoch to go home on first ship bound south. Demented white man brought on board by Indians, put in my cabin."

In the next day's record there appears the following: "Watched beside sick man all night; in intervals of sanity he tells a strange story, which I will write down to-day."

The 14th has the following:

"Wrote out story of stranger. See the back of this book."

And at the back of the book, written on paper cut from an old log of the "Champion," is the story that now, more than twenty-five years later, I tell you here:

On the evening of the 12th, I went on deck

to smoke and think of home, after a hard day's work getting the engines in shape for a siege. The ship was very quiet, half the crew being ashore, and some of the rest having gone in the boat with Captain Enoch to the "Enchantress," homeward bound and lying about half a mile below us. I am glad to say that Enoch's principal business aboard the "Enchantress" is to get me passage to San Francisco. I despise this kind of dreariness—rather be in state prison near the folks.

I sat on the rail, just abaft the stack, watching some natives handle their big canoes, when a smaller one came alongside. I noticed that one of the occupants lay at full length in the frail craft, but paid little attention until the canoe touched our side. Then the bundle of skins and Indian clothes bounded up, almost screamed, "At last!" made a spring at the stays, missed them, and fell with a loud splash into the water.

The Indians rescued him at once, and in a few seconds he lay like one dead on the deck. I saw at a glance that the stranger in Indian clothes was a white man and an American.

A pretty stiff dram of liquor brought him to slightly. He opened his eyes, looked up at the rigging, and closing his eyes, he murmured: "Thank God!—'Frisco—Polaria!"

I had him undressed and put into my berth. He was shaking as with an ague, and when his clothes were off we plainly saw the reason—he was a skeleton, starving. I went on deck at once to make some inquiry of the Indians about our strange visitor, but their boat was just disappearing in the twilight.

The man gained strength, as we gave him nourishment in small, frequent doses, and talked in a disjointed way of everything under the sun. I sat with him all night. Toward morning he seemed to sleep longer at a time, and in the afternoon of yesterday fell into a deep slumber, from which he did not waken for nearly twenty hours.

When he did waken, he took nourishment in larger quantities, and then went off into another long sleep. The look of pain on his face lessened, a healthy glow appeared on his cheek, and he slept so soundly that I turned in—on the floor.

I was awake along in the small hours of the morning, and heard my patient stirring, so I got up and drew the little curtain over the bulls-eye port—it was already daylight. I gave him a drink and a biscuit, and told him I would go to the cook's galley and get him some broth, but he begged to wait until breakfast time—said he felt refreshed, and would just nibble a sea biscuit. Then he ate a dozen in as many minutes.

"Did you take care of my pack?" he said eagerly, throwing his legs out of the berth, and looking wildly at me.

"Yes, it's all right; lie down and rest," said I; for I thought that to cross him would set him off his head again.

"Do you know that dirty old pack contains more treasures than the mines of Africa?"

"It don't look it," I answered, and laughed to get him in a pleasant frame of mind—for I hadn't seen nor heard of his pack.

"Not for the little gold and other valuable things, but the proofs of a discovery as great as Columbus made, the discovery of a new continent, a new people, a new language, a new civilization, and riches beyond the dreams of a Solomon——"

He shut his eyes for a minute, and then continued: "But beyond Purgatory, through Death, and the other side of Hell——"

Just here Enoch came in to inquire after his health, and sat down for a minute's chat. Enoch is first, last, and all the time captain of a whaler; he knows about whales and whale-hunters just as an engineer on the road knows every speck of scenery along the line, every man, and every engine. Enoch couldn't talk ten minutes without being "reminded" of an incident in his whaling life; couldn't meet a whaleman without "yarning" about the whale business. He lit his pipe and asked: "Been whaling, or hunting the North Pole?"

"Well, both."

"What ship?"

"The 'Duncan McDonald.'"

"The—the 'McDonald!'—why, man, we counted her lost these five years; tell me about her, quick. Old Chuck Burrows was a particular friend of mine—where is he?"

"Captain, Father Burrows and the 'Duncan McDonald' have both gone over the unknown ocean to the port of missing ships."

"Sunk?"

"Aye, and crushed to atoms in a frozen hell."

Enoch looked out of the little window for a long time, forgot his pipe, and at last wiped a tear out of his eye, saying, as much to himself as to us: "George Burrows made me first mate of the first ship he ever sailed. She was named for his mother, and we left her in the ice away up about the seventy-third parallel. He was made of the salt of the earth—a sailor and a nobleman. But he was a dare-devil—didn't know fear—and was always venturing where none of the rest of us would dare go. He bought the 'McDonald,' remodeled and refitted her after he got back from the war—she was more than a whaler, and I had a feeling that she would carry Burrows and his crew away forever——"

Eight bells rung just here, and Enoch left

us, first ordering breakfast for the stranger, and saying he would come back to hear the rest after breakfast.

As I was going out, a sailor came to the door with a flat package, perhaps six inches thick and twelve or fourteen square, covered with a dirty piece of skin made from the intestines of a whale, which is used by the natives of this clime because it is light and water-proof.

"We found this in a coil of rope, sir; it must belong to him. It must be mostly lead."

It was heavy, and I set it inside the door, remarking that here was his precious pack.

"Precious! aye, aye, sir; precious don't describe it. Sacred, that's the word. That package will cause more excitement in the world than the discovery of gold in California. This is the first time it's been out of my sight or feeling for months and months; put it in the bunk here, please."

I went away, leaving him with his arms around his "sacred" package.

After breakfast, Enoch and I went to the

little cabin to hear the stranger's story, and I, for one, confess to a great deal of curiosity. Our visitor was swallowing his last bowl of coffee as we went in. "So you knew Captain Burrows and the 'Duncan McDonald,'" said he. "Let me see, what is your name?"

"Alexander, captain of the 'Champion,' at your service, sir."

"Alexander; you're not the first mate, Enoch Alexander, who sat on a dead whale all night, holding on to a lance staff, after losing your boat and crew?"

"The same."

"Why, I've heard Captain Burrows speak of you a thousand times."

"But you were going to tell us about the 'Duncan McDonald.' Tell us the whole cruise from stem to stern."

"Let's see, where shall I begin?"

"At the very beginning," I put in.

"Well, perhaps you've noticed, and perhaps you have not, but I'm not a sailor by inclination or experience. I accidentally went out on the 'Duncan McDonald.' How old would you take me to be?"

"Fifty or fifty-five," said Enoch.

"Thanks, captain, I know I must look all of that; but, let me see, forty-five, fifty-five, sixty-five, seventy—seventy—what year is this?"

"Seventy-three."

"Seventy-three. Well, I'm only twenty-eight now."

"Impossible! Why, man, you're as gray as I am, and I'm twice that."

"I was born in forty-five, just the same. My father was a sea captain in the old clipper days, and a long time after. He was in the West India trade when the war broke out, and as he had been educated in the navy, enlisted at once. It was on one of the gunboats before Vicksburg that he was killed. My mother came of a well-to-do family of merchants, the Clarks of Boston, and—to make a long story short—died in sixty-six, leaving me considerable money.

"An itching to travel, plenty of money, my majority, and no ties at home, sent me away from college to roam, and so one spring morning in sixty-seven found me sitting lazily in the stern of a little pleasure boat off Fort Point in the Golden Gate, listlessly watching a steam whaler come in from the Pacific. My boatman called my attention to her, remarking that she was spick-and-span new, and the biggest one he ever saw, but I took very little notice of the ship until in tacking across her wake, I noticed her name in gold letters across the stern—'Duncan McDonald.' Now that is my own name, and was my father's; and try as I would, I could not account for this name as a coincidence, common as the name might be in the highlands of the home of my ancestors; and before the staunch little steamer had gotten a mile away, I ordered the boat to follow her. I intended to go aboard and learn, if possible, something of how her name originated.

"As she swung at anchor, off Goat island, I ran my little boat alongside of her and asked for a rope. 'Rope?' inquired a Yankee sailor, sticking his nose and a clay pipe overboard; 'might you be wantin' to come aboard?'

" 'Yes, I want to see the captain.'

" 'Well, the cap'en's jest gone ashore; his dingy is yonder now, enemost to the landin'. You come out this evenin'. The cap'en's particular about strangers, but he's always to home of an evenin'.'

" 'Who's this boat named after?'

" 'The Lord knows, stranger; I don't. But I reckon the cap'en ken tell; he built her.'

"I left word that I would call in the evening, and at eight o'clock was alongside again. This time I was assisted on board and shown to the door of the captain's cabin; the sailor knocked and went away. It was a full minute, I stood there before the knock was answered, and then from the inside, in a voice like the roar of a bull, came the call: 'Well, come in!'

"I opened the door on a scene I shall never forget. A bright light swung from the beams above, and under it sat a giant of the sea—Captain Burrows. He had the index finger of his right hand resting near the

North Pole of an immense globe; there were many books about, rolls of charts, firearms, instruments, clothing, and apparent disorder everywhere. The cabin was large, well-furnished, and had something striking about it. I looked around in wonder, without saying a word. Captain Burrows was the finest-looking man I ever saw—six feet three, straight, muscular, with a pleasant face; but the keenest, steadiest blue eye you ever saw. His hair was white, but his long flowing beard had much of the original yellow. He must have been sixty. But for all the pleasant face and kindly eye, you would notice through his beard the broad, square chin that proclaime the decision and staying qualities of the man."

"That's George Burrows, stranger, to the queen's taste—just as good as a degerrytype," broke in Enoch.

"Well," continued the stranger, "he let me look for a minute or two, and then said: 'Was it anything particular?'

"I found my tongue then, and answered: 'I hope you'll excuse me, sir; but I must confess it is curiosity. I came on board out of curiosity to——'

" 'Reporter, hey?' asked the captain.

" 'No, sir; the fact is that your ship has an unusual name, one that interests me, and I wish to make so bold as to ask how she came to have it.'

" 'Any patent on the name?'

" 'Oh, no, but I——',

" 'Well, young man, this ship—by the way, the finest whaler that was ever stuck together—is named for a friend of mine; just such a man as she is a ship—the best of them all.'

" 'Was he a sailor?'

" 'Aye, aye, sir, and such a sailor. Fight! why, man, fighting was meat and drink to him——'

" 'Was he a whaler?'

" 'No, he wa'n't; but he was the best man I ever knew who wa'n't a whaler. He was a navy sailor, he was, and a whole ten-pound battery by hisself. Why, you jest ort to see him waltz his old tin-clad gun-boat up agin one of them reb forts—jest naturally skeered 'em half to death before he commenced shooting at all.'

" 'Wasn't he killed at the attack on Vicksburg?'

" 'Yes, yes; you knowed him didn't you? He was a——'

" 'He was my father.'

" 'What? Your father?' yelled Captain Burrows, jumping up and grasping both my hands. 'Of course he was; darn my lubberly wit that I couldn't see that before!' Then he hugged me as if I was a ten-year-old girl, and danced around me like a maniac.

" 'By all the gods at once, if this don't seem like Providence—yes, sir, old man Providence himself! What are you a-doin'? When did you come out here? Where be you goin', anyway?'

"I found my breath, and told him briefly how I was situated. 'Old man Providence has got his hand on the tiller of this craft or I'm a grampus! Say! do you know I was wishin' and waitin' for you? Yes, sir; no more than yesterday, says I to myself, Chuck Burrows, says I, you are gettin' long too fur to the wind'ard o' sixty fur this here trip all to yourself. You ort to have young blood in this here enterprise; and then I just clubbed myself for being a lubber and not getting married young and havin' raised a son that I could trust. Yes, sir, jest nat'rally cussed myself from stem to stern, and never onct thought as mebbe my old messmate, Duncan McDonald, might 'a'done suthin' for his country afore that day at Vicks— say! I want to give you half this ship. Mabee I'll do the square thing and give you the whole of the tub yet. All I want is for you to go along with me on a voyage of discovery—be my helper, secretary, partner, friend—anything. What de ye say? Say!' he yelled again, before I could answer, 'tell ye what I'll do! Bless me if—if I don't adopt ye; that's what I'll do. Call me pop from this out, and I'll call you son. *Son!*' he shouted, bringing his fist down with a bang on the table. '*Son!* that's the stuff! By the bald-headed Abraham, who says Chuck Burrows ain't got no kin? The "Duncan McDonald," Burrows & Son, owners, captain, chief cook, and blubber cooker. And who the hell says they ain't?'

"And the old captain glared around as if he defied anybody and everybody to question the validity of the claims so excitedly made.

"We l, gentlemen, of course there was much else said and done, but that announcement stood; and to the day of his death I always called the captain Father Burrows, and he called me 'son,' always addressing me so when alone, as well as when in the company of others. I went every day to the ship, or accompanied Father Burrows on some errand into the city, while the boat was being refitted and prepared for a three-years' cruise.

"Every day the captain let me more and more into his plans, told me interesting things of the North, and explained his theory of the way to reach the Pole, and what could be found there; which fascinated me. Captain Burrows had spent years in the North, had noted that particularly open seasons occurred in what appeared cycles of a given number of years, and proposed to go above the eightieth parallel and wait for an open season. That, according to his figuring, would occur the following year.

"I was young, vigorous, and of a venturesome spirit, and entered into every detail with a zest that captured the heart of the old sailor. My education helped him greatly, and new books and instruments were added to our store for use on the trip. The crew knew only that we were going on a three-years' cruise. They had no share in the profits, but were paid extra big wages in gold, and were expected to go to out-of-the-way places and further north than usual. Captain Burrows and myself only knew that there was a brand-new twenty-foot silk flag rolled up in oil-skin in the cabin, and that Father Burrows had declared: 'By the hoary-headed Nebblekenizer, I'll put them stars and stripes on new land, and mighty near to the Pole, or start a butt a-trying.'

"In due course of time we were all ready, and the 'Duncan McDonald' passed out of the Golden Gate into the broad Pacific, drew her fires, and stopped her engines, reserving this force for a more urgent time. She spread her ample canvas, and stood away toward Alaska and the unknown and undiscovered beyond.

"The days were not long for me, for they were full of study and anticipation. Long chats with the eccentric but masterful man whose friendship and love for my father had brought us together were the entertainment and stimulus of my existence—a man who knew nothing of science, except that he was master of it in his own way; who knew all about navigation, and to whom the northern seas were as familiar as the contour of Boston Common was to me; who had more stories of whaling than you could find in print, and better ones than can ever be printed.

"I learned first to respect, then to admire, and finally to love this old salt. How many times he told me of my father's death, and how and when he had risked his life to save the life of Father Burrows or some of the rest of his men. As the days grew into weeks, and the weeks into months, Captain Burrows and myself became as one man.

" I shall never forget the first Sunday at sea. Early in the morning I heard the captain order the boatswain to pipe all hands to prayers. I had noticed nothing of a religious nature in the man, and, full of curiosity, went on deck with the rest. Captain Burrows took off his hat at the foot of the mainmast, and said:

" 'My men, this is the first Sunday we have all met together; and as some of you are not familiar with the religious services on board the 'Duncan McDonald,' I will state that, as you may have noticed, I asked no man about his belief when I employed him—I hired you to simply work this ship, not to worship God—but on Sundays it is our custom to meet here in friendship, man to man, Protestant and Catholic, Mohammedan, Buddhist, Fire-worshiper, and pagan, and look into our own hearts, worshiping God as we know him, each in his own way. If any man has committed any offense against his God, let him make such reparation as he thinks will appease that God; but if any man has committed an offense against his fellow-man, let him settle with that man now and here, and not worry God with the details. Religion is goodness and justice and honesty; no man needs a sky-pilot to lay a course for him, for he alone knows where the channel, and the rocks, and the bar of his own heart are—look into your hearts.'

"Captain Burrows stood with his hat in his hand, and bowed as if in prayer, and all the old tars bowed as reverently as if the most eloquent divine was exhorting an unseen power in their behalf. The new men followed the example of the old. It was just three minutes by the wheel-house clock before the captain straightened up and said 'Amen,' and the men turned away about their tasks.

" 'Beats mumblin' your words out of a book, like a Britisher,' said the captain to me; 'can't offend no man's religion, and helps every one on 'em.'

"Long months after, I attended a burial service conducted in the same way—in silence.

"In due course of time we anchored in Norton Sound, and spent the rest of the winter there; and in the spring of sixty-eight, we worked our way north through the ice. We passed the seventy-fifth parallel of latitude on July 4th. During the summer we took a number of whales, storing away as much oil as the captain thought necessary, as he only wanted it for fuel and our needs, intending to take none home to sell unless we were unsuccessful in the line of discovery—in that event he intended to stay until he had a full cargo."

Here our entertainer gave out, and had to rest; and while resting he went to sleep, so that he did not take up his story until the next day.

In the morning our guest expressed a desire to be taken on deck; and, dressed in warm sailor clothes, he rested his hand on my shoulder, and slowly crawled on deck and to a sheltered corner beside the captain's cabin. Here he was bundled up; and again Enoch and I sat down to listen to the strange story of the wanderer.

"I hope it won't annoy you, gentlemen," said he, "but I can't settle down without my pack; I find myself thinking of its safety. Would you mind sending down for it?"

It was brought up, and set down beside him; he looked at it lovingly, slipped the rude strap-loop over his arm, and seemed ready to take up his story where he left off. He began:

"I don't remember whether I told you or not, but one of the objects of Captain Burrows's trip was to settle something definite about the location of the magnetic pole, and other magnetic problems, and determine the cause of some of the well-known distortions of the magnetic needle. He had some odd, perhaps crude, instruments, of his own design, which he had caused to be constructed for this purpose, and we found them very efficient devices in the end. Late in July, we found much open water, and steamed steadily in a northwesterly course. We would find a great field of icebergs, then miles of floe, and then again open water.

The aurora was seen every evening, but it seemed pale and white.

"Captain Burrows brought the 'Duncan McDonald's' head around to the west in open water, one fine day in early August, and cruised slowly; taking a great many observations, and hunting, as he told me, for floating ice—he was hunting for a current. For several days we kept in the open water, but close to the ice, until one morning the captain ordered the ship to stand due north across the open sea.

"He called me into his cabin, and with a large map of the polar regions on his table, to which he often referred, he said: 'Son, I've been hunting for a current; there's plenty of 'em in the Arctic ocean, but the one I want ain't loafing around here. You see, son, it's currents that carries these icebergs and floes south; I didn't tell you, but some days when we were in those floes, we lost as much as we gained. We worked our way north through the floe, but not on the surface of the globe; the floe was taking us south with it. Maybe you won't believe it, but there are currents going north in this sea; once or twice in a lifetime, a whaler or passage hunter returns with a story of being drifted *north*—now that's what I want, I am hunting for a northern current. We will go to the northern shore of this open water, be it one mile or one thousand, and there—well, hunt again.'

"Well, it was in September when we at last got to what seemed the northern shore of this open sea. We had to proceed very slowly, as there were almost daily fogs and occasional snow-storms; but one morning the ship rounded to, almost under the shadow of what seemed to be a giant iceberg. Captain Burrows came on deck, rubbing his hands in glee.

"'Son,' said he, 'that is no iceberg; that's ancient ice, perpetual ice, the great ice-ring —palæcrystic ice, you scientific fellows call it. I saw it once before, in thirty-seven, when a boy; that's it, and, son, beyond that there is something. Take notice that that is ice; clear, glary ice. You know a so-called iceberg is really a snowberg; it's three-

"What seemed to be a giant iceberg . . ."
(*page* 282.)

fourths under water. Now, it may be possible that, that being ice which will float more than half out of water, the northern currents may go under it—but I don't believe it. Under or over, I am going to find one of 'em, if it takes till doomsday.'

"We sailed west, around close to this great wall of ice, for two weeks, without seeing any evidence of a current of any kind, until there came on a storm from the northwest that drove a great deal of ice around the great ring; but it seemed to keep rather clear of the great wall of ice and to go off in a tangent toward the south. The lead showed no bottom at one hundred fathoms, even within a quarter of a mile of the ice.

"It was getting late in the season, the mercury often going down to fifteen below zero, and every night the aurora became brighter. We sailed slowly around the open water, and finally found a place where the sheer precipice of ice disappeared and the shore sloped down to something like a beach. Putting out a sea-anchor, the 'Duncan McDonald' kept within a half-a-mile of this icy shore.

The captain had determined to land and survey the place, which far away back seemed to terminate in mountain peaks of ice.

"That night the captain and I sat on the rail of our ship, talking over the plans for to-morrow's expedition, when the ship slowly but steadily swung around her stern to the mountain of ice—the engines had been moving slowly to keep her head to the wind. Captain Burrows jumped to his feet in joy. 'A current!' he shouted; 'a current, and toward the north, too—old man Providence again, son; he allus takes care of his own!'

"Some staves were thrown overboard, and, sure enough, they floated toward the ice; but there was no evidence of an opening in the mighty ring, and I remarked to Captain Burrows that the current evidently went under the ice.

"'It looks like it did, son; it looks like it did; but if it goes under, we will go over.'

"After we had taken a few hours of sleep, the long-boat landed our little party of five men and seven dogs. We had food and drink for a two weeks' trip, were well armed, and carried some of our instruments. It appeared to be five or six miles to the top of the mountain, but it proved more than thirty. We were five days in getting there, and did so only after a dozen adventures that I will tell you at another time.

"We soon began to find stones and dirt in the ice, and before we had gone ten miles, found the frozen carcass of an immense mastodon—its great tusks only showing above the level; but its huge, woolly body quite plainly visible in the ice. The ice was melting, and there were many streams running towards the open water. It was warmer as we proceeded. Dirt and rocks became the rule, instead of the exception, and we were often obliged to go around a great boulder of granite. While we were resting, on the third day, for a bite to eat, one of the men took a dish, scooped up some sand from the bottom of the icy stream, and 'panned' it out. There was gold in it: gold enough to pay to work the ground. About noon of the fifth day, we reached the summit of the mountain, and from there looked down the other side—

upon a sight the like of which no white men had ever seen before.

"From the very summits of this icy-ring mountain the northern side was a sheer precipice of more than three thousand feet, and was composed of rocks, and rocks only, the foot of the mighty crags being washed by an open ocean; and this was lighted up by a peculiar crimson glow. Great white whales sported in the waters; huge sea-birds hung in circles high in the air; yet below us, and with our glasses, we could see, on the rocks at the foot of the crags, seals and some other animals that were strange to us. But follow the line of beetling crags and mountain peaks where you would, the northern side presented a solid blank wall of awful rocks, in many places the summit overhanging and the shore well under in the mighty shadow. Nothing that any of us had ever seen in nature before was so impressive, so awful. We started on our return, after a couple of hours of the awe-inspiring sight beyond the great ring, and for full two hours not a man spoke.

" 'Father Burrows,' said I, 'what do you think that is back there?'

" 'No man knows, my son, and it will devolve on you and me to name it; but we won't unless we get to it and can take back proofs.'

" 'Do you think we could get down the other side?'

" 'No, I don't think so, and we seem to have struck it in the lowest spot in sight. I'd give ten years of my life if the 'Duncan McDonald' was over there in that duck pond.'

" 'Captain,' said Eli Jeffries, the second mate, 'do you know what I've been thinkin'? I believe that 'ere water we seen is an open passage from the Behring side of the frozen ocean over agin' some of them 'ere Roosian straits. If we could get round to the end of it, we'd sail right through the great Northwest Passage.'

" 'You don't think there is land over there somewhere?'

" 'Nope.'

" 'Didn't take notice that the face of your

"passage" was granite or quartz rocks, hey? Didn't notice all them animals and birds, hey?——'

" 'Look out!' yelled the man ahead with the dog-sledge.

"A strange, whirring noise was heard in the foggy light, that sounded over our heads. We all dropped to the ground, and the noise increased, until a big flock of huge birds passed over us in rapid flight north. There must have been thousands of them. Captain Burrows brought his shot-gun to his shoulder and fired. There were some wild screams in the air, and a bird came down to the ice with a loud thud. It looked very large a hundred feet away, but sight is very deceiving in this white country in the semi-darkness. We found it a species of duck, rather large and with gorgeous plumage.

" 'Goin' north, to Eli's "passage" to lay her eggs on the ice,' said the captain, half sarcastically.

"We reached the ship in safety, and the captain and I spent long hours in trying to form some plan for getting beyond the great ice-ring.

"'If it's warm up there, and everything that we've seen says it is, all this cold water that's going north gets warm and goes out some place; and rest you, son, wherever it goes out, there's a hole in the ice.'

"Here we were interrupted by the mate, who said that there were queer things going on overhead, and some of the sailors were ready to mutiny unless the return trip was commenced. Captain Burrows went on deck at once, and you may be sure I followed at his heels.

"'What's wrong here?' demanded the captain, in his roaring tone, stepping into the midst of the crew.

"'A judgment against this pryin' into God's secrets, sir,' said an English sailor, in an awe-struck voice. 'Look at the signs, sir,' pointing overhead.

"Captain Burrows and I both looked over our heads, and there saw an impressive sight, indeed. A vast colored map of an unknown world hung in the clouds over us—a mirage from the aurora. It looked very near, and was so distinct that we could distinguish polar bears on the ice-crags. One man insisted that the mainmast almost touched one snowy peak, and most of them actually believed that it was an inverted part of some world, slowly coming down to crush us. Captain Burrows looked for several minutes before he spoke. Then he said: 'My men, this is the grandest proof of all that Providence is helping us. This thing that you see is only a picture; it's a mirage, the reflection of a portion of the earth on the sky. Just look, and you will see that it's in the shape of a crescent, and we are almost in the center of it; and, I tell you, it's a picture of the country just in front of us. See this peak? See that low place where we went up? There is the great wall we saw, the open sea beyond it, and, bless me, if it don't look like something green over in the middle of that ocean! See, here is the "Duncan McDonald," as plain as A, B, C, right overhead. Now, there's nothing to be afraid of in that; if it's a warning, it's a good one—and if any one wants to go home to his mother's, and is old enough, *he can walk!'*

"The captain looked around, but the sailors were as cool as he was—they were reassured by his honest explanation. Then he took me by the arm, and, pointing to the painting in the sky, said: 'Old man Providence again, son, sure as you are born; do you see that lane through the great ring? There's an open, fairly straight passage to the inner ocean, except that it's closed by about three miles of ice on our side; see it there, on the port side?'

"Yes, I could see it, but I asked Captain Burrows how he could account for the open passages beyond and the wall of ice in front; it was cold water going in.

" 'It's strange,' he answered, shading his eye with his hand, and looking long at the picture of the clear passage, like a great canal between the beetling cliffs. All at once, he grasped my arm and said in excitement, pointing towards the outer end of the passage: 'Look!'

"As I looked at the mirage again, the

great mass of ice in front commenced to slowly turn over, outwardly.

" 'It's an iceberg, sir, only an iceberg!' said the captain, excitedly, 'and she is just holding that passage because the current keeps her up against the hole; now, she will wear out some day, and then—in goes the "Duncan McDonald"!'

" 'But there are others to take its place,' and I pointed to three other bergs, apparently some twenty miles away, plainly shown in the sky; 'they are the reinforcements to hold the passage.'

" 'Looks that way, son, but by the great American buzzard, we'll get in there somehow, if we have to blow that berg up.'

"As we looked, the picture commenced to disappear, not fade, but to go off to one side, just as a picture leaves the screen of a magic lantern. Over the inner ocean there appeared dark clouds; but this part was visible last, and the clouds seemed to break at the last moment, and a white city, set in green fields and forests, was visible for an instant, a great golden dome in the center remaining

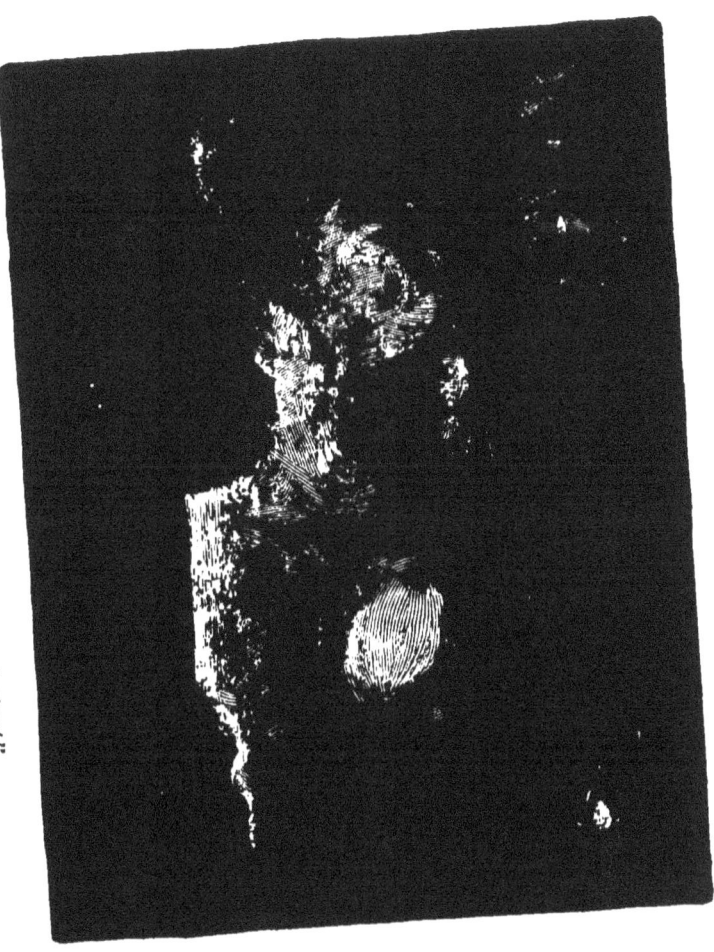

"A white city . . . was visible for an instant."
(page 292.)

in view after the rest of the city was invisible.

"'A rainbow of promise, son,' said the captain.

"I looked around. The others had grown tired of looking, and were gone. Captain Burrows and myself were the only ones that saw the city.

"We got under way for an hour, and then stood by near the berg until eight bells the next morning; but you must remember it was half dark all the time up there then. While Captain Burrows and myself were at breakfast, he cudgeled his brains over ways and means for moving that ice, or preventing other bergs from taking its place. When we went on deck, our berg was some distance from the mouth of the passage, and steadily floating away. Captain Burrows steamed the ship cautiously up toward the passage; there was a steady current coming out.

"'I reckon,' said Eli Jeffries, 'they must have a six-months' ebb and flow up in that ocean.'

"'If that's the case, said Captain Burrows, 'the sooner we get in, the better;' and he ordered the 'Duncan McDonald' into the breach in the world of ice.

"Gentlemen, suffice it to say that we found that passage perfectly clear, and wider as we proceeded. This we did slowly, keeping the lead going constantly. The first mate reported the needle of the compass working curiously, dipping down hard, and sparking—something he had never seen. Captain Burrows only said: 'Let her spark!'

"As we approached the inner ocean, as we called it, the passage was narrow; it became very dark and the waters roared ahead. I feared a fall or rapid, but the 'Duncan McDonald' could not turn back. The noise was only the surf on the great crags within. As the ship passed out into the open sea beyond, the needle of the compass turned clear around and pointed back. 'Do you know, son,' said Captain Burrows, 'that I believe the so-called magnetic pole is a great ring around the true Pole, and that we just passed it there? The whole inside of this mountain looks to me like rusted iron instead of stone, anyhow.'"

Here our story-teller rested and dozed for a few minutes; then rousing up, he said: "I'll tell you the rest to-morrow; yes, to-morrow; I'm tired now. To-morrow I'll tell you about a wonderful country; wonderful cities; wonderful people! I'll show you solar pictures such as you never saw, of scenes, places, and people you never dreamed of. I will show you implements that will prove that there's a country where gold is as common as tin at home—where they make knives and forks and stew-pans of it! I'll show you writing more ancient and more interesting than the most treasured relics in our Sanscrit libraries. I'll tell you of the two years I spent in another world. I'll tell you of the precious cargo that went to the bottom of the frozen ocean with the staunch little ship, 'Duncan McDonald;' of the bravest, noblest commander, and the sweetest angel of a woman that ever breathed and lived and loved. I'll tell you of my escape and the hell I've been through. To-morrow——"

He dozed off for a few moments again.

"But I've got enough in this pack to turn the world inside out with wonder—ah, what a sensation it will be, what an educational feature! It will send out a hundred harum-scarum expeditions to find Polaria—but there are few commanders like Captain Burrows; he could do it, the rest of 'em will die in the ice. But when I get to San Fran——. Say, captain, how long will it take to get there, and how long before you start?"

Enoch and I exchanged glances, and Enoch answered: "We wa'n't goin' to 'Frisco."

"Around the Horn, then?" inquired the stranger, sitting up. "But you will land me in 'Frisco, won't you? I can't wait, I must——"

"We're goin' *in*," said Enoch; "goin' north, for a three-years' cruise."

"North!" shouted the stranger, wildly. "Three years in that hell of ice. Three years! My God! North! North!"

He was dancing around the deck like a maniac, trying to put his pack-loop over his head. Enoch went toward him, to tell him how he could go on the "Enchantress," but he looked wildly at him, ran forward and sprang out on the bowsprit, and from there to the jib. Enoch saw he was out of his mind, and ordered two sailors to bring him in. As they sprang on to the bow, he stood up and screamed:

"No! No! No! Three years! Three lives! Three hells! I never——"

One of the men reached for him here, but he kicked at the sailor viciously, and turning sidewise, sprang into the water below.

A boat, already in the water, was manned instantly; but the worn-out body of another North Pole explorer had gone to the sands of the bottom where so many others have gone before; evidently his heavy pack had held him down, there to guard the story it could tell—in death as he had in life.

THE END

www.ingramcontent.com/pod-product-compliance
Lightning Source LLC
Chambersburg PA
CBHW031907220426
43663CB00006B/799